STATE OF VE[RMONT]
DEPARTMENT OF
MIDSTATE REGION
578 PAINE TPKE N
BERLIN VT 05602

D0883582

WITHDRAWN

LADY DIANA SPENCER
Princess of Wales

LADY DIANA SPENCER
Princess of Wales

Nancy Whitelaw

MORGAN
REYNOLDS
Incorporated

Greensboro

LADY DIANA SPENCER: *Princess of Wales*

Copyright © 1998 by Nancy Whitelaw

Photo Credits:

AP/Wide World Photos
Globe Photos, Inc.
Rex Features

Library of Congress Cataloging-in-Publication Data
Whitelaw, Nancy
  Lady Diana Spencer: Princess of Wales / Nancy Whitelaw. —1st ed.
    p. cm.
  Includes bibliographical references and index.
  Summary: A biography of the Princess of Wales, beginning with her birth and including
her death in 1997.
    ISBN 1-883846-35-8
      1. Diana, Princess of Wales, 1961— —Juvenile literature. 2. Princessess—Great
Britian—Biography—Juvenile literature. [1. Diana, Princess of Wales, 1961—   .
2. Princesses. 3. Women—Biography.] I. Title
DA591. A45D5377 1998
941.085' 092—dc21
[B]

                                                                    98-5378
                                                                        CIP

Printed in the United States of America
First Edition

Dedicated to
Megan Christine Torrey
with lots of love

Contents

Princess Diana

Chapter One

———————————————

———————

"...but she could be obstinate..."
                    —a nanny talking about Diana

In 1961, Johnnie and Frances Spencer awaited the birth of their third child, the one that had to be a boy. The couple had just about everything else a British couple could want. They had two daughters, Sarah, aged six, and Jane, aged four. They had titles—Viscount and Viscountess Althorp—and a grand home with a full-time staff of six in an exclusive neighborhood which included royalty. They had a family tradition of wealth and social class that reached back to the fifteenth century. But in this year of 1961, they had no heir to carry on the family name. If no son survived their deaths, all those special class distinctions and privileges would be scattered among males who were cousins and other more distant relatives.

The seven-pound twelve-ounce infant arrived on July 1, a beautiful and healthy baby. But it was a girl. Obviously, their chosen name of Charles was not appropriate. It took the parents a week to find a name for this baby. They decided on Diana in memory of a Spencer ancestor and Frances because this was her mother's name. Diana Frances Spencer was christened in a neighborhood church in near-by Sandringham. Her godparents were relatives and friends of the family.

Diana's home was a ten-bedroom mansion leased to her grandfather Fermoy through a friendship with King George V. The estate included an outdoor swimming pool, tennis courts, a cricket field, and a fine collection of rare books and art. The little girl learned to play by herself much of the time. Her older sisters were busy with home tutors many mornings, and her mother was often busy with social engagements. Still, Diana always had Ally around. Ally was a nanny who taught Diana to pay attention to outward appearances. Diana learned to be well-dressed and neat, to speak when spoken to, chew with her mouth closed, sit up straight, and shake hands with guests.

In 1964, the long-awaited male Spencer was born. Charles Viscount Althorp was christened at Westminster Abbey, not at the Sandringham church as Diana was. Queen Elizabeth II of the royal house of Windsor was one of his godparents. Diana missed her brother's christening party. She had disobeyed her nanny, slid down some steps on a metal tea tray, and hurt her head.

Two of little Diana's favorite people were her baby brother and her Grandmother Spencer. Diana loved taking care of Charles. She fed him, bathed him, and played with him. Ally remembers about Diana, "She has always loved babies." She also loved her grandmother, Countess Spencer, who often told Diana of her adventures visiting the poor and the sick.

Diana learned that she could sometimes avoid confrontation

and still do what she wanted to do. One of her nannies remembers how she scolded her for not eating the crust on her bread. The nanny was delighted when she no longer saw crust on Diana's plate. She was less than delighted when she found piles of crust stuffed up under the ledge of the nursery table. Another nanny says: "Diana could not be called a difficult child but she could be obstinate."

Queen Elizabeth II, her husband Prince Philip, and their children sometimes stayed at the family castle in the village of Sandringham. They exchanged visits with the Spencers. Prince Andrew, the Queen's son, was closest in age to Diana, and she played with him while his mother visited with the adults. Andrew's brother Charles was twelve years older than Diana and was scarcely interested in the younger children except to show his superiority as big brother. Diana became comfortable with the royal family.

Like her siblings, Diana was aware that her parents did not get along well. Sometimes she hid behind a door or a piece of furniture when she heard her parents arguing. Just as frightening were the times when the couple did not speak to each other. They had little in common but the children. Her father, Johnnie, enjoyed solitary hobbies like hunting and fishing. Her mother, Frances, enjoyed socializing, meeting people, and lively conversation. Also, there was a twelve-year difference in their ages, with Johnnie being the older. Outside of Park House, the Spencers put on a united and happy front. They had been brought up with a strict code of public behavior, and they would not allow their emotion to break this code.

In 1967, Sarah and Jane were away at boarding school when Frances and Johnnie agreed to a trial separation. Frances took Diana and Charles with her to a flat in London. Diana adjusted pretty well and enjoyed going to a day school where she did particularly well in art. In December, Frances took the children back to Park House to celebrate Christmas as a family. Johnnie refused to let the children leave after the holidays.

Diana's memory of the end of the holiday began as she sat on the bottom of the stairs at Park House. She didn't watch; she only listened as her father made seemingly endless trips to the car with her mother's possessions. Then she heard the car door slam, and her mother was gone. Later, she heard a rumor that her mother had fallen in love with another man. He was Peter Shand Kydd, a married man with children.

In the eyes of many friends and relatives, including even Frances' mother, Frances was unfaithful to her husband and negligent toward her children. To other friends and relatives, Frances was a misunderstood wife who left her home because her husband was a difficult man. As for Diana, she recalls, "My parents were busy sorting themselves out. I remember my mother crying. Daddy never spoke to us about it. We could never ask questions."

In the divorce case, Frances charged Johnnie with cruelty. He charged her with adultery. Johnnie won custody of the children in April 1969. Charles, Diana, Sarah, and Jane would be under the care of the man who had insisted that their mother

After her mother and father divorced, young Diana Spencer spent a great deal of time alone or with her many animals on the family estate.

leave their house. To make up for the difficult family situation, Johnnie promised to make more time for his children. The next month Frances married Peter Shand Kydd.

Her father gave Diana a tan and white guinea pig named Peanuts and a calf. Diana loved taking care of her pets. She cared for them both alive and dead. She flushed dead fish down the toilet. Other dead animals she placed in shoeboxes, buried them, and marked each grave with a cross. For her seventh birthday, her father rented a camel from the local zoo, and the party guests took turns riding it across the garden. She feared horses after she fell off her pony, Romany, and broke her arm.

Despite their fun, the children were unhappy about being away from their mother. Their father hired several different nannies for them. But the children were suspicious of anyone who seemed to take their mother's place, and they misbehaved until the nanny quit or was fired. Diana made a resolution soon after her parents divorced. She told her nanny, "I'll never ever marry unless I really love someone. If you're not really sure you love someone, then you might get divorced. I never want to be divorced."

Every weekend the children visited their mother on the 100-acre farm where she lived with her new husband. There they enjoyed fishing, swimming, sailing, and picnics.

Like most boys and girls of her social class, Diana was sent away to boarding school. Before she left for Riddlesworth Hall, nine-year-old Diana and her mother went shopping for the proper school outfit—gray pleated skirt, gray knee socks, gray

Diana loved to take care of her baby brother Charles.

coat, and a cherry-red headband. At school, she was awakened each morning at 7:30 by a cowbell. She and the other students made their beds and met for prayers before classes began. Each student was allowed to bring a small pet to school. Diana's guinea pig, Peanuts, won first prize in the Fur and Feather section of a holiday pet show.

Her parents visited on alternate weekends, always bringing treats. In her letters to them, Diana told them what food to bring. High on her lists were a big chocolate cake and ginger cookies.

Although she didn't like many of her classes, Diana did like English history. Perhaps this was partly because her ancestry included ambassadors, knights, lords, earls, and members of Parliament. Many Spencers had worked for royalty in high-ranking positions. Her father supervised the royal stables for both George VI and Queen Elizabeth. Her grandmother Fermoy was a Lady of the Bedchamber to the Queen Mother (Elizabeth II's mother). Diana's family had brought her up to believe that the strength of England lay in the royal family. Prime ministers, members of Parliament, and other government officials would come and go with the whim of English voters. But the royal family was a constant symbol unaffected by the political, social, or economic climate.

Her classmates remembered her as having a special interest in food. She used to sneak out of the dorm to buy sweets. And she rose to the challenge when friends dared her to eat as much as she could hold.

Students at Riddlesworth were encouraged to be good citizens. Every weekend Diana and other students visited with elderly women, sometimes cleaning, sometimes shopping, sometimes simply chatting, and listening. She also visited at a mental hospital where she worked with individual patients, trying to find a way to communicate with each one. At the end of her first year at Riddlesworth, Diana won a trophy for helpfulness. Her principal remembered, "She was awfully sweet with the little ones."

Diana did poorly in English literature and language, history, geography, and art. This was especially difficult for her because both Jane and Sarah had earned good academic records. Diana did well in swimming, diving, and tennis. But she believed that her sisters had done better. She could pick out pieces on the piano after hearing them only once. But she was embarrassed to play since her grandmother and her sister Sarah were excellent pianists. To make things worse, she grew tall quickly and worried about being the tallest girl in her class.

She became an excellent ballet dancer because of her natural grace and her willingness to learn. Some nights she sneaked out of bed to practice by herself in the big school hall. "It always released tremendous tension in my head," she said. She won several prizes for her dancing. But she knew that she could not become a professional dancer because she was too tall. She was quick to sign up for every school trip to the Coliseum or Sadler's Wells ballet performances.

In 1975, after graduating from Riddlesworth, Diana enrolled

at the West Heath School in Kent. Both Sarah and Jane had been students there. Jane had excelled both in sports and in academics; Sarah had been expelled for drinking because, she said, she wasn't interested in school. Diana got along well. One of her roommates described her as "...someone with whom you could never be bored." Another classmate said that Diana was always ready to help anybody. Her principal remembered her as an ordinary student—sometimes well-behaved, sometimes giggling, and talking when she was not supposed to. As she had done at Riddlesworth, Diana spent some time in volunteer work. She visited the elderly, and she played with handicapped children weekly.

Like thousands of other young British girls, Diana tacked up a photo of Charles, Prince of Wales, in her dormitory room. He was tall, handsome, rich, and a bachelor. He would become king of England when his mother, Queen Elizabeth II, died or abdicated, and his wife would become queen of England. Newspapers pictured him dating one glamorous woman after another; he publicly quashed ideas of marriage to any of them.

In 1975, Diana's grandfather Spencer died. Her father became the 8th Earl Spencer. Sarah, Jane, and Diana became Ladies. Her father moved the family into the Spencer home at Althorp, about 100 miles from London. Diana spent many happy vacation days there, swimming in the pool, driving her brother's beach buggy, dancing, reading romances by Barbara Cartland, and filling up on the sweets she could not get at school.

Diana spent most of her school holidays in the outdoors.

Raine Lewsiham was a frequent visitor to Althorp. The Spencer children disliked Raine for her flamboyant manner, loud speech, elaborate hairdo and flashy clothes. Sometimes the girls gleefully chanted to themselves "Raine, Raine, go away." To Diana, one good thing about Raine was that her mother was Barbara Cartland, one of her favorite novelists. Most of the family was shocked and dismayed when Johnnie suddenly announced that he had married Raine in a private ceremony in July 1977.

Raine, now Countess Spencer, made sweeping changes in the Spencer home. She fired much of the staff. She restored and repainted walls and ceilings, furniture and art work. She even changed family customs. A typical change was Raine's Christmas rule that no one could open a present without first getting Raine's permission. Diana and the other children no longer enjoyed vacations at home as they had before their father's marriage.

At West Heath, sixteen-year-old Diana failed many of her school tests. She took them again—and failed again. Her behavior record was no better. One of the punishments for breaking rules was weeding the garden. "I became a great expert in weeding," recalls Diana. When asked what she wanted to do with her life, Diana laughed and said she would like to marry Prince Charles and become the Princess of Wales. Others laughed too. They had all read the papers and knew about Charles and Lady Jane Wellesley, Charles and Camilla Parker,

Charles and Lucia Santa Cruz—and Charles and many other women.

Diana enrolled at the Institut Alpin Videmanette, a finishing school in Switzerland where Sarah had been a student. She did not enjoy the classes in French, dressmaking, and cooking. She loved the skiing. Thinking more seriously about what she wanted to do with her life, she decided that she wanted to work with children in some way. This gave her a reason to disobey the rule that students must speak French at all times. What good would knowledge of French do her when she was working with kids? Soon after she enrolled, she started sending letters home, begging to be allowed to return to England. After a few months, her family relented. Diana left school.

Chapter Two

"You should be with somebody to look after you."
—Diana to Charles

Back in England, Diana stayed with a family friend as nanny to the children with some cooking and cleaning responsibilities. But she wanted a more independent living style. She begged her mother to let her live in London with two roommates. It made sense, Diana reasoned, to live in her mother's city apartment since Frances stayed in Scotland most of the time. Her mother agreed, partly because Diana was so insistent and partly because Diana's two sisters were already living in London. Jane worked as an editorial assistant for the fashion magazine *Vogue* and Sarah worked for a real estate agency.

London was glorious. As often as she could, Diana went to ballet performances. She waited at the stage door to collect autographs of the dancers. She and her roommates frequently went shopping and to movies and nightclubs together. Their favorite pop music was by the Police, Neil Diamond, and Abba. Like her school roommates, these friends often spoke of Diana's love of humor. They also spoke of her love of chocolate— chocolate cake, chocolate candy, chocolate anything. Each of the girls had dates and boyfriends. None seemed serious. They often borrowed from each other's closets; mixing and matching outfits with a great deal of fun and laughing.

Diana worked because she wanted to, not because she had to. Besides a large inheritance from her grandmother, she had generous parents. She signed up with a temporary employment agency and soon worked at many different jobs—nanny, helper at private parties, cleaning lady. She took a ten-week course in cooking and then accepted jobs cooking and serving food. She also taught dancing to children ages two to nine. She liked the casual life of a temporary worker. She wore jeans a lot, and often cycled to her various jobs.

Diana happily went from one job to another. She loved working as helper in a pre-school. Besides giving lots of affection and attention to the kids, she mixed paint, cut paper, and generally was jack-of-all-trades for the busy teachers. A fellow worker remembers Diana saying "Please, God, may I have only daughters. Little boys are so rough."

Diana's sister Sarah sometimes dated Prince Charles. She went to some of his polo matches, they skied together in Switzerland, and they attended balls and parties together. But Sarah was not well. Already suffering from an alcohol problem, she also became a victim of anorexia, an eating disorder called slimmers in England. Her weight dropped from 112 pounds to seventy-seven pounds in just a few months. Sarah believed that part of her problem was her parents' divorce and part was her disappointment in her own love life. "In such circumstances," she said, "you behave like an alcoholic. You will just not admit that there is a problem. Worse, you end up believing you are beautiful, looking so thin."

In February 1980, Diana attended a royal house party at Sandringham. Prince Charles no longer dated Sarah, and again rumors flew about who might finally convince the bachelor prince to settle down. Diana didn't pay much attention to the talk. She simply had a great time socializing and dancing.

In July, Diana went to another royal house party. There she sat next to Prince Charles. He was still grieving over the recent assasination of the Earl of Mountbatten, a great uncle to whom he had been particularly close. Diana had been to the funeral and remembered Charles' mourning. "You looked so sad when you walked up the aisle at the funeral," she told him "My heart bled for you. You should be with somebody to look after you."

After that day, Charles invited Diana out to a music perfor- mance, for supper at Buckingham Palace, and to a special celebration on the royal yacht, *Britannia.* Then he asked her to spend a weekend at Balmoral Castle in Scotland. On the castle grounds, she stayed with her sister Jane, whose husband, Robert, was a private secretary to Queen Elizabeth II. Charles called her every day to invite her to a walk, a barbecue, a chat with friends. He asked her to go salmon fishing with him. Diana went, although she was not interested in fishing. When she spotted the lenses of binoculars aimed at them, she realized that photogra- phers were spying on them. She put on a headscarf and an old cap and escaped to her sister's home.

Prince Charles and Diana's sister, Lady Sarah Spencer, attending a polo match.

Prince Charles with his beloved great uncle the Earl of Mountbatten. This photo was taken a few month before Mountbatten's assasination.

Aggressive photographers had earned a special name in 1973 when one of them harassed former First Lady Jacqueline Onassis. Photographer Ronald Galella was the first to be declared a paparazzo legally. He was required to stay at least twenty-five feet away from Mrs. Onassis. Now Diana felt the sting of the paparazzi.

After that weekend, rumors spread about Diana and Charles. Diana, who was quickly nicknamed Shy Di by the media, received phone calls at all hours from reporters. She never knew when she might hear a nearby click of a camera. They were ever ready with flashbulbs popping as she walked to and from the nursery and when she was outside with the children. A few photographers tried to sneak onto the nursery property to take pictures. The rumors hinted at a fairy tale of the twentieth century. Diana was nineteen years old, happily working in a pre-school, shy, and beautiful. Charles was thirty-three, born to be king, a pilot of warplanes, an international polo player, captain of a Royal Navy ship.

In October, Charles took Diana to Highgrove, a Gloucestershire home he had bought recently. The squarish plain-fronted mansion had about twenty rooms, almost 350 acres of land, and excellent stables. A lush wildflower garden bordered the driveway. Charles asked her opinion about re-decorating the eight-bedroom house. Although they were developing a warm friendship, she continued to address him as Sir as she had been taught. He called her Diana.

Sometimes Charles took her to the home of Camilla Parker-

Diana worked as a nanny in the period before her engagement to Prince Charles.

Bowles and Major Andrew Bowles. The couple were long-time friends of Charles and were gracious in their entertaining.

Charles told Diana that he felt sorry for Camilla. Reporters who had linked his name with hers sometimes hounded her. Diana did not tell him that she experienced the same problems.

The press became bolder about Charles and Diana. One reporter declared that there could be no doubt about the coming marriage of Diana and Charles. His reasoning was that the Prince needed a young and beautiful wife who could produce an heir—male, of course—to the throne. Besides, her family background included the necessary aristocratic status to marry a king-to-be. He assumed that any young woman would be thrilled to marry Prince Charles.

In November, a newspaper article in the *Saturday Mirror* reported that police had spotted Diana sneaking into a royal railroad car to spend the night with Charles. Diana, Charles, and the royal family insisted that the story was not true. Diana said: "I have never been on that train. I have never ever been near it." Diana's roommates confirmed her story.

Diana's mother wrote a letter to the *The London Times*: "May I ask the editors of Fleet Street, whether in the execution of their jobs, they consider it necessary or fair to harass my daughter daily, from dawn until well after dusk?" The royal family demanded an apology from Bob Edwards, editor of the *Sunday Mirror*. Edwards refused. Some thought that royal pressure would be exerted to see that he was removed from his position. When he was not, suspicion grew that the story was true.

Prince Charles with Camillia Parker in 1975.

That same month, a reporter asked Diana if she was going to marry Charles. She responded, "I really don't know.... I can't say anything. I just can't say anything."

As more and more stories and photos appeared, members of Parliament considered a motion to publicly criticize the reporters and photographers. The motion did not pass.

Diana learned to fool the press in several different ways. Once she used torn bed sheets to lower her suitcase out a window where reporters were not watching. Then she sneaked out a back door. Another time she ran out the fire exit of a store to evade them. Still other times, her roommate Carolyn drove Diana's car to decoy the press away from the apartment. As soon as Carolyn and the pursuing reporters were out of sight, Diana walked quickly away in the opposite direction. One day, when photographers were chasing her, she stopped the car and jumped out, running into the crowds to escape.

In January, Charles called Diana from Switzerland where he was on a skiing trip. He told her that he had an important question for her when he returned to England the next month. She and her roommates guessed what that question was. Surely it must be a proposal. Diana was undecided. Her heart told her to say yes. But she had some questions. Was he truly in love with her? Could she adapt to a royal life? How important was his relationship with Camilla?

The next month, Charles invited Diana to a candlelight dinner in Windsor Castle. The room was decorated with photos of British royalty—the Queen and Philip, Queen Victoria and her grandchildren. He told her that he had missed her on the skiing trip and that he wanted to marry her. He warned her that her life would not be her own after the marriage. Some reports of that conversation say that Diana made light of the proposal, even giggled. Other reports say that she answered yes promptly. In any case, the answer was yes.

Charles asked her father for Diana's hand. Royal jewelers sent her a tray of engagement rings. She chose an eighteen-carat white gold ring with a large oval sapphire surrounded by fourteen diamonds believed to be worth about $54,000.

On February 24, Charles and Diana's engagement was formally announced from Buckingham Palace. This was the first time that a Prince of Wales had arranged his own marriage. Houses of

The recently engaged Prince Charles and Diana with Queen Elizabeth.

Parliament cheered. The HMS *Bronington*, Charles' minesweeper, fired a twenty-one-gun salute. The stock market soared.

Diana's father arrived outside Buckingham Palace with his camera. "I wanted to photograph the photographers," he explained. Her stepmother, Raine, said, "What will make the marriage so good is that Diana is a giver." Barbara Cartland said about Diana, "...she's got a strong personality, vivacious but strong. Strength within herself. And magic..."

Diana was to live with the Queen Mother, Elizabeth's mother, at the royal residence, Clarence House. The Queen Mother would help her get used to royal customs and responsibilities. Leaving her London flat, Diana left her roommates a note: "For God's sake, ring me up—I'm going to need you."

Amidst the flurry of news about the engagement ring, the wedding plans, and the declarations of love, an insistent questioning rose about the future of the thousand-year-old monarchy in England. The publicity surrounding Charles and Diana was part of a growing change in royal tradition. Kings and queens had lived in stately dignity, most often behind castle walls, always a class apart from their subjects, always in mysterious splendor.

Those royal walls began to crack in the twentieth century. As modern methods of communication brought news to more and more people, the press began to push at the cracks. Feature articles about the royal family helped to sell newspapers and magazines. One of the biggest stories of the century was about King Edward VIII in 1936. As king, he was forbidden to marry a person who was divorced. Edward fell in love with twice-divorced Wallis Simpson and gave up his throne in order to marry her.

Queen Elizabeth II had a part in opening the royal wall in 1953. She allowed a public television broadcast of her coronation. That was the end of privacy for the royal family. The press delighted readers with articles and photos about the fascinating romances of Queen Elizabeth's sister, Princess Margaret. They let out the word that Prince Philip, husband of Queen Elizabeth II, went out drinking with his friends. They snapped photos of fourteen-year-old Prince Charles sipping brandy in a pub.

On a more serious note, political editorials questioned the

monarchy. What was the value of the royal family? Did all the expense of royal trappings do anything worthwhile for the public? One reporter wrote: "Nobody can seriously pretend that the royal round of gracious boredom ...is politically useful or morally stimulating."

People in the streets questioned it too. Did they need or want the pomp and majesty of the royal family? Would they rather see the royal money spent on increasing employment, helping the needy and other causes? Did they truly respect those to whom they curtsied and bowed?

The obvious next question: What would Diana bring to the royal tradition when she became queen? Did she have the appropriate upbringing, style, and temperament to follow in the footsteps of past queens? Were the British people ready—and eager—for a new kind of queen, a high-spirited woman?

The country faced a decline in the economy, race riots, hostility toward Prime Minister Margaret Thatcher, and doubts about the importance of the royal family. Diana brought lightness and a charm with her smile, her beauty, her romance with Charles, and the wedding plans.

Following the engagement announcement, Charles worked on a busy schedule of royal visits all over the world. Frequently asked about Diana, he apologized that she had not accompanied him on the tour. He explained that she had many duties now and "I think she would drop from sheer exhaustion before the wedding" if she had come with him. At a dinner with President and Mrs. Ronald Reagan, the American president told Charles that he too was twelve years older than his wife, Nancy.

Diana had to adjust to many changes in her life without Charles to help her. She had to become accustomed to the two detectives who followed her everywhere she went. She had to accept the fact that at least once a day a story about her was printed in a London newspaper. She had to adapt to the formal schedule of meals and visiting at Clarence House. She continued to greet both Elizabeth and the Queen Mother with a full curtsy and to address both as Ma'am.

Her formal wardrobe consisted of one long dress, one silk shirt, and a smart pair of shoes. Much had to be bought before she was ready to enter a life that might include four changes of formal wardrobe in one day. A few times she sneaked away from the press to meet with London editors of *Vogue* magazine. They discussed her entire wardrobe beginning with underwear and ending with make up and hairstyle. They talked about her posture. They gave her hints on how to overcome her shyness. But they could not give her self-confidence. She told her friends, "I wish I could believe what they tell me. But I still feel awful on so many occasions."

When asked if she loved Charles, Diana quickly answered that she did. When Charles was asked if he loved Diana, he nodded and said, "Whatever 'in love' means." Charles' valet commented, "Diana seemed bowled over by Charles. She worshiped the ground he walked on. He [Charles] would respond to her affection and kiss her, but not as enthusiastically and fervently as she wanted."

Chapter Three

"I'll be there at the altar for you."

—*Charles to Diana*

Diana appeared frequently outside Buckingham Palace where crowds waited to see her. On one occasion, she realized that one of the spectators was blind. She held out her left hand, saying, "Do you want to feel my engagement ring?" People often gave her flowers. She took them with thanks and smiles. As she passed on down the lines of crowds, she sometimes stuck a carnation or other blossom into the buttonhole of a spectator.

The public adulation and the press insistence wearied Diana. She lost weight in the three months before the wedding. Some people say that it was during this time that Diana became subject to bulimia nervosa, a disease in which the victim overeats and then induces vomiting. Her former roommate Carolyn said, "She wasn't happy, she was suddenly plunged into all this pressure and it was a nightmare for her." Still she did some serious thinking about the ceremony. She and the dean of Westminster Abbey agreed to omit the word "obey" from the marriage vows. The dean said, "...if there's going to be a dominant partner, it won't be settled by this oath."

The wedding dress had to be created. Designers David and Elizabeth Emanuel said, "We want to make her look like a fairy princess." They were determined to keep details of the gown a secret. Those who worked on the bodice were not allowed to talk with those who worked on the skirt; those who worked on the sleeves were not allowed to listen to those who worked on the train. Because they feared that a "spy" might find out something about the gown by going through the trash, the Emanuels burned every scrap of unusable cloth each day.

All over the world, women wore clothes like Diana's, had their hair cut, shaped and streaked like hers, and bought souvenirs of the engagement. A popular magazine, *Tatler*, wrote an article about how girls could look more like Diana. Newspapers ran competitions for Di look-alikes and had headlines when Diana's hairdresser added more highlights.

Diana was lonely and bored some of the time. She relieved her boredom a little by chatting with the staff in the kitchens and taking private ballet and tap dancing lessons. Her already weak self-confidence was shattered by the arrival of a package in her office at the palace. Inside was a bracelet engraved with the letters "F" and "G." Diana knew right away that the letters stood for Fred and Gladys, the nicknames Charles and Camilla had given each other. Obviously, the package had been delivered to her by mistake. When she asked Charles about it, he said simply that the gift was a token of friendship for Camilla.

While Diana was bored, the royal staff was in a panic about the wedding. Extensive preparations were necessary to take care of the twenty-five hundred invited guests from all over the world—kings and queens, princes and princesses, staff members of royal households, relatives and friends.

Scotland Yard drew up plans to have a policeman every four feet along the carriage route as well as sharpshooters on roofs. An officer in the Welsh Guards prepared the coach that Queen Elizabeth had used at her wedding. The baker in charge of the wedding cakes said he had no written recipe—it was all in his head. The largest of the finished raisin/cherry/rum cakes would weigh almost seventy pounds and stand four-and-one-half feet high. The Emanuels faced a small emergency when they learned that Diana had lost so much weight that the gown no longer fit as they had planned. They quickly made adjustments.

Charles entertained at a traditional stag party the night before the wedding. Diana asked that she be allowed to spend that night with her three former roommates. The royal answer was no; she was to have a quiet dinner with her mother, grandmother, and the Queen Mother.

Charles sent Diana a small ring embossed with the royal symbol. He enclosed a card that said, "I'm so proud of you and when you come up I'll be there at the altar for you tomorrow."

The wedding day, July 29, 1981, was declared a government holiday with factories and offices closed. All over the country, people had parties, bonfires, and parades. Streets filled with tens of thousands of people. Two tons of explosives set off a display of twelve thousands rockets. A five-hundred-member military band played while a choir of Welsh guards sang.

The doors of St. Paul's Cathedral opened at 9:00, and the twenty-five hundred guests were seated by 9:30. At 10:22, the queen left the palace in a procession of closed carriages. At 10:30, Prince Charles' two-car procession left Buckingham Palace. At the same time, the bells of St. Paul's Cathedral began a half-hour of chiming. At 10:35, Diana and her father left Clarence House in a coach called the Glass Carriage because three large glass panels gave spectators an excellent view of the interior. Her hand-embroidered white train flowed over the red leather seats. All along the two-mile route to the church, over a million people cheered, waved, applauded, and held up signs with slogans like *Britain Needs Charlie and Di.*

At the church, a footman in scarlet and gold opened the carriage door and Diana stepped onto a red carpet. The crowd went wild as they got their first full-length look at the bride. The dazzling tiara, a Spencer family heirloom, glittered with sequins. Her dress was ivory silk taffeta and lace with a scoop neckline and full sleeves. Diana and her father walked up the twenty-four steps to the door of the church.

As the cathedral clock struck eleven, the wedding processional started, a blend of trumpets and the seven-thousand pipe cathedral organ. Diana and her father moved down the aisle following eleven clergy dressed in red and silver, five bridesmaids and two boy pages. Her twenty-five-foot train, the longest in English wedding history, covered most of the red carpet behind her.

Three and a half minutes later, she was face to face with

The wedding of the century, July 29, 1981.

Charles, who waited at the altar in his Royal Navy uniform, one hand on the hilt of his sword. He grinned and whispered, "You look wonderful." "Wonderful for you," she whispered back.

After congregational singing, the dean of St. Paul's spoke the familiar words, "Dearly beloved, we are gathered here..." Then came more singing; a reading from Corinthians 13: "Love is patient; love is kind and envies no one...."; and an address by the archbishop of Canterbury. After the seventy-minute ceremony, the Archbishop declared "I pronounce that they be man and wife together." Outside, crowds heard the statement over the loudspeaker and cheered. All over the world, probably 750 million people had watched the wedding on television.

Outside, Diana and Charles rode together in an open carriage as crowds roared and shouted and threw rose petals and confetti along the route. They chanted "Lady Di, Lady Di, Lady Di." The bells of St. Paul's rang for almost four hours.

Once the royal family was inside Buckingham Palace, the crowd shouted for the newly weds to appear on the balcony. Most insistent were the shouts of "We want Di, we want Di..." When the couple appeared, the crowd changed their shouts to "Kiss her, kiss her, kiss her." Charles did. The crowd went wild.

At 4:40, the couple stepped into a carriage trimmed with heart-shaped balloons and a sign scrawled in lipstick that announced *Just Married*. Diana wore a tangerine suit, and Charles a gray one. They were driven to the royal train.

For the honeymoon, they went first to Broadlands, about ninety miles from London. This estate was a sixteenth century

A happy Diana and Charles on their honeymoon in Scotland.

sixty-room mansion on six thousand acres. They were almost alone—only six servants were present. After a couple of days at Broadlands, Charles piloted them to Gibraltar in an old propeller Royal Air Force plane. There they climbed aboard the royal yacht *Britannia* for a Mediterranean cruise. The royal suite that spanned four decks included a wine cellar, a garage for their Rolls Royce, and a theater. The couple swam, windsurfed, and loafed in the glassed-in sitting room. Twenty-one officers and two hundred crewmen went along on this phase of the honeymoon.

They left the *Britannia* in August to fly to Balmoral Castle in Scotland. They would stay with Queen Elizabeth until their own home at Kensington Palace was ready. At Balmoral, the royal couple decided to appease some of the photographers who had been hounding them. They scheduled a photo session on the banks of the River Dee. They posed for hundreds of photos—he in a kilt and she in a brown tweed check suit.

Then they settled down to open some of the ten thousand wedding presents that were stored away. The wide array included saddles, paintings, a picnic basket, a potato shaped like a heart, a bag of coffee beans, and a seven-foot-high birdhouse. Although staff was available to write acknowledgments and thank-yous, Diana replied to many of the gift-givers personally.

In October, she spent three days on an official tour in Wales. This might have been a difficult tour. Unemployment in Wales was up to sixteen percent, and the economy was down. Traditionally, many Welsh had seen the British as snobs who believed that they were superior. Even the weather was against her as dark and cloudy skies scattered rain in her path.

To the surprise of many, crowds lined the streets to meet this new princess as she passed by shops, trailer courts, and run-down coal mines. She smiled and waved, and people in the streets waved and smiled back. They wanted to touch her, to talk to her, and to listen to her voice. She answered their comments easily and naturally. She asked some how far they had come for the procession. She asked others if they had been waiting long for her. She expressed surprise and delight at their loyalty to her. She graciously accepted hundreds of gifts— among them flowers, poems, and a Welsh heifer.

In Cardiff, she gave her first public speech as Diana, Princess of Wales. When she uttered a phrase in Welsh, the crowd roared their approval of her accent. As one spectator put it, Diana "speaks it like an angel, she does."

Chapter Four

"I feel totally out of place here."
—*Diana to her former roommate*

Despite the success of the wedding, Diana's adjustment to a royal life was difficult. She could not get used to the police following her from room to room, even waiting outside the bathroom for her. She did not want them around while she shopped, visited friends, or went for a drive. Yet the police had been trained that they must do exactly that. Once she tried to refuse to allow a royal security guard to accompany her on a drive. "I don't need you, thank you," She told him. He replied, "I'm sorry, but we're part of your life now."

Formal dinners at Balmoral sometimes lasted three hours. She was expected to sit beside strangers, talk about whatever they wanted to talk about, and to be knowledgeable and charming at all times. She felt left out of the sophisticated talk and family jokes. She felt uncomfortable with the tradition that she must be addressed at first meeting as "Your Royal Highness" and in subsequent references referred to as "Ma'am." She wrote to one of her former roommates: "I feel totally out of place here...I sometimes feel so small, so lonely, so out of my depth."

She longed for the bachelor girl apartment where she and her friends had lounged around feasting on pizza or other fast food, and laughed a lot. She felt a yearning to return to the pubs and restaurants where she had had so much fun.

She was expected to attend many official functions—concerts, dinners with other royalty, memorial celebrations, and public appearances arranged so people could see her. Her favorite type of public appearance was called a walkabout—a stroll through streets and shops, shaking hands, chatting with people in the crowd. But the royal staff insisted the formal meetings were perhaps more important. Sometimes she refused to follow the official schedule. Some Diana-watchers say that these first months marked a dramatic change in her. They said that she felt increasingly concerned about her role as a royal. They also said that she was worried about the never-ending gossip about Charles and Camilla. She could think of no one to turn to with these problems. Several doctors and psychologists prescribed a number of tranquilizers. She resisted their advice because she thought that she needed sympathy and warmth, not medication. Her weight fell drastically.

Charles had many more official duties than Diana did. He was patron of 147 societies, head of the Duchy of Cornwall, and had to make himself available to endless callers and meetings. He supported a job creation project in Liverpool, Birmingham, and other cities. He helped to make funds available to people under twenty-five for self-help projects. He launched Youth Business Initiative, an organization to help young unemployed people start their own businesses. He was a director of the Prince's Trust, an organization that supported many different charities. He spoke of a determination to help any individual who was "...looking for other ways of doing things."

The pattern of Charles' life was determined at his birth. He was Prince of Wales and when his mother was no longer queen, he would become king. Through tradition, training, and role modeling by his mother, he had learned not to show emotion in public. This "stiff upper lip" attitude was a symbol of the strength of the royalty. Charles could not understand Diana's emotional reactions.

He asked one of his polo pals, Oliver Everett, to help Diana. Everett had been one of Charles' secretaries and knew all about royal obligations. Everett gained Diana's confidence. He told her what people to meet and whom to avoid, how to greet people according to their rank and status, and what subjects to talk about with different guests. Diana learned, but Queen Elizabeth believed that she should adjust more quickly. So she sent members of her staff to discuss with Diana what the queen perceived as weaknesses in her daughter-in-law's behavior. Diana did not take these criticisms easily.

Diana became tired of Everett's continual lessons, and she grew to believe that he, like her mother-in-law, was too picky. She put a note on Charles' desk. In huge letters she had written: "Oliver must go." Charles was reluctant. He believed that Everett was doing exactly what was necessary with the princess. Besides, he was an old friend. Charles and Diana fought frequently and loudly about the situation. Charles did not dismiss Everett, and Diana retaliated by refusing to participate in some of the social events Everett planned for her.

On November 5, 1981, Diana announced that she was pregnant. The Buckingham Palace announcement of the pregnancy set off another wave of Diana cheers. All over the country, people applauded the news, drank toasts to the baby-to-come, and made bets on the sex of the infant. Of course, it was hoped that the child was a boy, an heir to the throne. However, Diana was still young, and if she did not produce a male this time, surely she would try again. Reporters and photographers doubled their efforts to create news about Diana, who was already the most photographed woman in the world.

As the photographers continued to harass, the queen came to Diana's defense. She called a meeting of editors at Buckingham Palace and asked them to let Diana have some privacy. Some say that she did this out of genuine concern for Diana. Others say that she did it out of concern for the royal tradition of extreme privacy for the royal family. In any case, there was little or no change in press coverage. No editor could meet his competition without full coverage of Diana.

Diana was delighted to be pregnant, unlike the royal women who gave birth before her. In the mid-1800s, Queen Victoria had described her pregnancy as "that miserable lump" and she stayed out of public view until after the birth. When Princess Elizabeth was pregnant with Charles, reporters said merely she was in an "interesting condition." Also unlike royalty before her, Diana spoke with her obstetrician about having as natural a birth as possible. Elizabeth told Diana that royal women always had their babies delivered in the privacy of the palace. Diana insisted her baby would be born in a hospital.

With the pregnancy, Diana had less energy. She tried to explain to Charles that she simply could not keep up with the schedule outlined for her. Charles said only that the royal show must go on. She complained to his valet: "Can't he [Charles] understand that I need him to look after me? I feel he's abandoned me." She received no help.

A widely circulated rumor says that when Charles refused to comfort Diana, she threatened suicide. The story continues that Charles did not believe her and that she threw herself down a staircase. Still another story disputes this suicide attempt completely, saying that Diana had simply lost her footing on the stairs. In any case, the fetus was not affected by the fall.

In February, photographers followed Charles and Diana to the Bahamas. An editor and his photographer put on jungle gear to sneak up and take photos of Diana in a bikini. They published them. Again the royal family complained, and again the editors refused to admit that they had done anything wrong.

Diana and Charles were given an apartment at Kensington Palace, just down the road from her sister Jane. With gas lights and quiet courtyards, the red brick Kensington complex looked like an elegant English village. Three royal families lived there besides Diana and Charles—the prince and princess of Kent, Princess Margaret and her daughter Lady Sarah Armstrong-

Jones, and the duke and duchess of Gloucester. Charles and Diana's apartment covered several stories and included three reception rooms and a nursery. Diana decorated the nursery with some toys from her own childhood and filled the rest of the room with some of the two thousand gifts that arrived from all over the world. The high point of the room was a canopied four-poster bed of golden pine.

Diana was delighted to live near Jane. They enjoyed many happy moments together. Jane's closeness helped especially when Charles was off on his frequent appointments and trips.

Diana also enjoyed the company of Sarah Armstrong-Jones. The two young women had much in common—childhood in a broken home, interest in dancing, and less-than-spectacular marks in school. They lounged around in jeans, watched John Travolta movies, and ate pizza and other fast food.

Diana adopted some new ways to avoid the press. A few times, with the aid of a headscarf and oversize sunglasses, she escaped photographers long enough to enjoy shopping trips and lunch with her friends. She loved being anonymous. She told a friend, "I hate all this heel-clicking and bowing and not being called plain Diana anymore."

But she would never be plain Diana again. The press criticized every one of Diana's public actions. If she was seen coming out of a department store with boxes, she was extravagant. If she came out with nothing, she was too picky. When she wore a mink coat, animal activists protested. If she left a public appearance because she didn't feel well, she was rude.

Besides these criticisms, the press also picked up on public attitudes toward Diana's wardrobe and life-style. Newspaper readers saw photos of Diana dressed in new and glamorous outfits. Especially during a period when the economy was down, citizens were quick to complain about subsidizing a lavish royal lifestyle. While millions were struggling to pay for food and shelter, they resented expenditures for fancy clothes, vacations, extravagant homes, and expensive entertainment.

The morning of June 21, 1982, Diana woke Charles to tell him that it was time to go to the hospital. They arrived at St. Mary's Hospital a little after five a.m. Crowds gathered outside the building when they discovered that Diana was in labor. Standing in the rain, they listened to their portable radios, waiting for the first official bulletin announcing the birth. Just after nine in the evening, someone hung a hand-printed sign outside the hospital—*It's a Boy!* The seven-pound, two-ounce infant was healthy. Less than twenty-four hours after the birth, Diana, Charles, and the yet-unnamed infant left the hospital.

A few days later, Charles announced that the baby had a name. He would be William Arthur Philip Louis George. Sixty guests attended the christening at Buckingham Palace. William wore the white silk christening dress worn by Queen Victoria's first child. The archbishop of Canterbury sprinkled over William's head baptismal water flown in from the Jordan River.

After the ceremony, William demonstrated his fine pair of lungs. His nanny whisked him away. The guests enjoyed a champagne lunch, complete with the top tier saved from the

Diana and Prince William on the day of his Christening, August 4, 1982.

wedding cake as tradition dictated.

Diana was determined not be an absentee mother, as her mother had been. Charles and Diana agreed to do as much diapering, feeding, and bathing as they could, although they had a full-time nanny.

Diana often cut her appointments short to be at home with her child. She expected Charles to do the same. But Charles did not understand Diana's vision of family life with a baby. When he was a child he had been cared for by nannies most of the time. He had seen his mother on schedule for thirty minutes each morning and sometimes for thirty minutes each evening. He accepted the fact that his mother was generally too busy with royal duties to care for him.

Many Britons agreed with Charles. They remembered photos of Elizabeth greeting her sons after a several-month international tour. The little boys did not rush to her and hug her. They greeted her with a handshake. This was proper parent and child behavior for royal families. Charles and Diana were unable to discuss their conflict because of a basic disagreement about parental responsibilities. They could only argue.

Charles and Diana asked editors to take fewer photos. The editors refused, saying that they needed lots of pictures to sell their newspapers. However, Diana sometimes managed to avoid the press for several days at a time. Without daily news about her, reporters used rumors to create stories. They wrote that Charles and Diana argued about the price of her clothes. They also wrote that she was anorexic. Another report said that she was continually high-strung, pushed almost to the limit by royal pressure. Still another said that she was a shop-aholic with an unquenchable interest in buying clothes. Other stories said that she was bored stiff because Charles was off shooting deer most of the time, leaving her alone. Other reports had Diana seeing a succession of psychotherapists, psychologists, dream-analyzers, doctors, and other professional consultants.

A cycle of misery set in for both Diana and Charles. Diana felt tired and lonely. The worse she felt, the less she ate. The less she ate, the more tired she felt. She complained about Charles' lack of attention and sympathy. On the other side, Charles accepted a heavier schedule of appearances to make up for Diana's absences. As he worked harder, he became more distressed with Diana's attitudes. As he became more distressed, he stayed away from home more often.

Gradually, and with some reluctance, Diana returned to public life. She visited hospitals, speaking with every patient who wanted to talk to her and attended charity dinners. She drove around in her Ford Escort, accompanied by a detective and bodyguard. But she always left time for William.

Once she and Charles thrilled a crowd with their antics. At a charity variety show, Charles appeared on stage dressed as Romeo from Shakespeare's *Romeo and Juliet*. The spotlight turned on Diana in her royal box—and she was there dressed as Juliet. She threw down a rope for Charles to climb. He produced a ladder. The audience laughed until the tears rolled down their faces. Charles rushed up the ladder and publicly embraced his wife while the audience cheered.

At Christmas 1982, Charles, Diana, and six-month-old William posed for publicity photos. William was chubby, handsome, and serious. "I'm sorry he's not all that smiley today," said Charles. "We will probably get all those child specialists saying we handled him wrong."

One cold day Diana went out to greet crowds in front of the palace for a look at the royal family. She told them she was touched that they had stood outside for so long just to meet them.

The following spring, Diana and Charles planned a tour of Australia and New Zealand. This trip was not simply a public relations tour, and they would stay several weeks. The new prime minister of Australia, Robert Hawke, had talked about cutting all ties to the British monarchy by the year 2000. Charles' responsibility was to do what he could to soften Hawke's decision. Wanting to be prepared for all kind of situations, Diana selected two hundred outfits for the trip. A big problem arose when she insisted that William, less than one year old, would accompany them. The royal family objected strenuously. The queen had always left their children with the staff at home, in order not to detract from the royal purpose of the visit. Diana obviously should do the same. She could not do that, Diana said, because she loved playing with him so much.

Here again, the differences in Diana and Charles' goals in life caused conflict. Charles, like the rest of the royal family, believed that duty to country came first. Diana believed that her first responsibility was to her children.

Chapter Five

"The Royal Family is never on holiday."

—journalist to readers

Diana overrode the royal objections. William traveled with them. When his father and mother were busy, William spent his time in a home in eastern Australia with his nanny. Every few days the parents returned to William to enjoy him and to relax. Diana had won a battle, but she did not win the war. The royal staff declared that children would never again be allowed on royal tours. Diana declared that under those circumstances, she would not go on a long tour again, "Children cannot be left for that length of time at their age," she told Charles.

Diana charmed the children in Australia, as she charmed children everywhere. In Alice, a town of eighteen thousand, she and Charles answered students' questions over a School of the Air educational broadcast station. Diana and Charles walked along the streets, waving, smiling, and often stopping. She chatted with some mothers about her baby and theirs, about her clothes, about their everyday problems. In Brisbane more than one hundred thousand people crowded around to see her.

Everywhere they went, Charles applauded the connection

between Australia and the British monarchy. But his verbal message was not as strong as Diana's appeal. He publicly admitted that Diana was upstaging him: "I have come to the conclusion that it really would have been easier to have had two wives. Then they could cover both sides of the street and I could walk down the middle directing operations."

For some short walkabouts, they took William. The baby seemed to love the crowds. He showed his teeth, crawled, and stood on his own feet for a moment. At one point he stuck out his tongue at a Maori, a traditional Maori greeting.

All in all, the visit was highly successful, but both the prince and princess were tired. Now they were ready for a vacation, far from photographers and reporters. A photographer from the *Daily Mirror* said this was impossible: "Well, the Royal Family is never on holiday. The world wants to *know*. I really think she'd like to be just Diana Spencer, and just go around like that. Well, she can't. Never again."

Still, they tried. They chose a castle in Liechtenstein that could be reached only by one road and was surrounded by a fifteen-foot-thick wall. Less than an hour after they arrived at the castle, forty reporters and photographers had registered at a nearby hotel. A helicopter carrying three photographers flew low enough to take photos of them as they skied. Photographers caught them eating lunch at a restaurant. Charles grinned and said, "Now I'm going to blow my nose for everyone to photograph." He did—and the photographers snapped the picture. Then Charles struck a bargain with them. If they would leave the couple alone for the rest of the lunch, they could take photos as they left the restaurant. But when that time came, Diana refused to smile or even to raise the ski hat that covered part of her face. Charles could not persuade her to do so. He apologized to the press.

Apparently, Diana felt the pressure more keenly than Charles did. For most of her life, Diana had been on the other side of publicity. She had been the hero-worshiper, the avid reader of gossip in the newspapers, and an enthusiastic member of cheering crowds. Prince Charles had been under public scrutiny ever since the moment he was born. As reporters noted her increasingly curt remarks and her attempts to escape interviews, questions arose about her personality and about her ability to fill her role as a member of the royal family. Newspaper headlines competed against each other to tell the "real" story: *Daily Express*—Diana behaved "like a spoilt brat"; several papers—"Diana eighty percent certain to have breakdown." They brought up the possibility of her anorexia and her tendency to weep easily. Diana insisted that she was not depressed. She said that she wept easily because this was part of her personality, not a physical or emotional problem.

Charles gave up trying to help Diana to become accustomed to her role. In 1983 he had Everett transferred to a new job as royal librarian. More and more frequently, they toured separately. Once while Diana visited poverty-stricken areas in Glasgow, Scotland, Charles worked as a farmhand, milking cows and repairing fences. When he left the farm, he remarked that he felt that being on a farm restored his sanity.

The royal staff scheduled an eighteen-day tour of Canada for the two of them. Diana said she wanted to stay home with William. She was told that she had to go. She went, but she wanted to call William every day on the trip. The couple greeted crowds who cheered at the top of their lungs. They planted trees, toured town halls, participated in Klondike celebrations. Diana visited several hospitals. In each one, she sat on beds and spoke to every patient who wanted to visit with her.

Newspaper, radio, and TV articles reported the popularity of the couple, especially of twenty-two-year-old Diana. Then one reporter on the Halifax *Daily News* broke a promise not to report on royal remarks made privately. He wrote that the princess agonized over the attention from the press. He said Diana had told him that she agonized when they wrote critical stories. She hoped she would get over this problem in five or ten years.

Back in England, Diana kept every morning free to be with William. She tried to keep the evening hours from six to eight o'clock free so that she could bathe him, get him ready for bed, and read to him. Charles and Diana argued about William's schooling. Charles believed that the boy should be schooled at home for the first few years just as he had been. Diana wanted William to gain from the socialization of schools like the kindergarten in which she had worked.

Interest in Diana's clothes and looks continued with the "Di look" of simple suits and hats with veils. Women asked their hairdressers for "Di-lights" to streak their hair like Diana's.

Charles had little interest in his clothes except for his one hundred uniforms. He had eight different navy uniforms as well as Welsh Guard dress, including kilts, scarlet tunics, and the khaki pullovers of informal barracks' dress.

A serious question arose—could bodyguards and special police keep the couple safe from kidnapping or other attack? There was no question about the potential danger. In 1981, would-be assassins had tried to kill both the pope and President Reagan. Just recently, a man had attempted to kidnap Princess Anne only yards from Buckingham Palace. Another man broke into Buckingham Palace and succeeded in getting into the queen's bedroom before he was apprehended. Diana and Charles took a series of lessons in security. They learned how to brace themselves in case they were tied up. This bracing might make it possible to untie their bonds secretly. They learned to use a .38 Smith and Wesson. They took lessons on how to avoid terrorist attacks and how to extricate themselves if they were caught. For further security, there was a 'safe room' at Highgrove with steel-lined walls to which they could escape.

By late 1983, Diana was pregnant again. She was under less pressure to produce a boy, although many hoped that she would have a son just in case something happened to William.

William grew strong and happy. His nanny admitted that he needed constant attention. He had dropped many things down the toilet—Diana's makeup, Charles' shoes, his own toys. The staff at Highgrove was warned not to leave anything on a low table or chair. Both his father and his mother admitted that he often broke his toys—and anything else he found. They disagreed on basic parenting, however. Diana saw the baby as a little child who should be encouraged to enjoy life. Charles saw him as a future king, in need of constant training.

On September 5, their second son was born. They named the child Henry Charles Albert David George, but they told the press that he would be called Harry. The christening was a happy one. William charmed the group by hugging his brother.

Diana begged Charles to spend more time with her and their two sons. For a few months, he stayed closer to home. Then his father and mother reminded him of his national obligations. That was the end of Charles' attempt to fit into Diana's ideas about family responsibilities.

Relatives, friends, and the press reported that Diana had many problems. That she went on eating sprees, sometimes eating a whole pudding or a complete meat pie at one sitting. She was especially fond of shepherd's pie, a meat concoction topped with mashed potatoes. She called this dish "mince n' mash mush." Another problem discussed was Diana's problems with the household staff. One published report noted that there had been nine major staff turnovers in just a few years. Some watchers blamed Diana, saying that she was hard to please.

She kept a busy schedule. She became involved with many charities—visiting victims, asking about research, and finding out what work was being done. She comforted mothers whose babies had died from Sudden Infant Death syndrome. She played with children at a home for neglected youngsters. She

Diana insisted that she have time to spend with her sons.

visited with the unemployed. She became a patron of Birthright, an organization that raised funds for research into problems of stillbirth, infant death, and infertility. One national organizer said of Diana's work in maternity wards: "The Princess has helped enormously with fund-raising. But the lift she gives to other young mums when she visits maternity wards is every bit as valuable as the extra money she brings in." When Diana supported a charity, that organization immediately gained favor in the eyes of the public. She attracted stars from all over the world—pop stars, rock musicians, playwrights, comedians— who gave shows to make money for charitable causes.

Charles, too, kept up a heavy schedule of appearances and speeches but he found time to relax in his garden, play polo, ski, and skin dive. He also wrote a children's book, *The Old Man of Lochnagar*, about a grouchy man who seeks adventure. It begins: "Not all that long ago, when children were even smaller and people had especially hairy knees, there lived an old man of Lochnagar...." When he had free time, Charles retreated frequently to his gardens and his study at Highgrove.

The different schedules of the royal couple echoed the differences in their personalities. Their problems arose from more than simply the twelve-year gap in ages. She liked ballet, and he did not; he liked opera, and she accompanied him only to be polite. She liked pop music; he liked classical. She liked television's *Dynasty* and *Dallas*; he seldom watched television. She had only a few close friends; he had many friends. Diana disliked formal social entertaining; Charles considered formality a necessary and proper aspect of royal life. Diana hated any form of hunting; Charles loved shooting and hunting. Diana wanted their sons to go to primary school where they would meet lots of other kids; Charles wanted them to have a governess in Kensington Palace for the first few years, just as he had.

Some speculated Diana was no longer useful to the royal family after she produced two sons. In fact, she have been an embarrassment because she took attention away from Charles and because her speech and actions were unpredictable. These ideas brought up more conflict, both in the royal family and in the eyes of British citizens. Could Diana properly serve her roles as Princess of Wales and later as queen? If she could not, what could be done about it?

Perhaps the most dreaded question of all was: Could the monarchy survive a divorce? The Church of England might issue a waiver that would allow Charles to divorce Diana. But when he became king, Charles would automatically become the head of the Church of England. Would the hierarchy of the church accept a divorced man, with or without a waiver, as head of that church? Would parishioners accept him as their leader?

Although the press and public worried about Diana's future, Diana found a new self-confidence. She knew for sure that she was a crowd-pleaser. She believed that she did not need constant instructions and training from Charles, Everett, Elizabeth, household staff, or her bodyguards. She could—and would— create her own role. She became more flamboyant in dress, and she smiled more and chatted more in crowds.

Charles found himself turning in the opposite direction. He was bored. Until he became king—and there was no indication that Elizabeth would abdicate soon—there would be no change in his role. He was annoyed with playing second fiddle to Diana. He began to spend more time on his farm.

Diana kept two journals. One was embossed with the royal seal and noted all her official engagements—teas, banquets, tours, etc. A typical week included such diverse activities as working out with dancers from the English National Ballet, greeting an audience in her drawing room at Kensington, meeting with a cardinal, and spending a day at a charity. Diana's secretaries sometimes inscribed MOTG, meaning Morally Obliged To Go, after events at which the queen had specifically asked for Diana's attendance.

In her private diary, embossed with her own coat of arms, she wrote the details of events that she considered private. They might include playing tennis, shopping, working out with a videotape, jogging around Kensington Gardens, playing with the children, dinner, and bridge parties with her friends. A constant priority in her schedule was time with her boys. She took them to school each morning and was at home when they returned. On the calendar, she highlighted their activities— school plays, ends of terms, outings, etc.—in green ink.

Diana went to a psychic who used astrology to help save marriages. After the first visit at which Diana told the psychic all about her personal problems, the two met regularly. The psychic explained to Diana that her star chart showed patterns that could lead her to rise from despair. Diana told a friend that the psychic suggested that she use her own marital problems to figure out positive ways to help.

Diana toured the United States in the fall of 1985. In Springfield, Virginia, she went to a J.C. Penneys and she chatted with executives and clerks and admired British-made clothes.

By early 1986, Diana was convinced that Charles no longer loved her if, in fact, he ever had. She often cried herself to sleep at night, worrying about the future. A story went around that one night Diana took a huge dose of paracetemol, also known as acetaminophen, a pain reliever and fever reducer. Then she thought about William and Harry. She rushed to the bathroom where she forced herself to vomit. Then she called Charles and told him what she had done. He immediately called a doctor who found that the vomiting had taken care of the medication. Was this an attempt at suicide? Or was it a cry of help to Charles?

Reporters and royal staff watched Diana closely on a trip to Japan that same year. They saw that she ate little more than a salad in a whole day. The chefs tried in vain to tempt her with more food. However, during that same trip, she won admiration and applause for her public appearances. She had taken a few lessons in Japanese, and she learned common phrases for words like *grateful, pleased, happy,* and *thrilled.* When she stood before a crowd and said, "Domo arigato gozaimashita" (Thank you very much), she won the hearts of the 125 million Japanese who watched her live and on television.

Chapter Six

"Anywhere I see suffering, that is where I want to be"
—*Diana in an AIDS clinic*

Diana kept a secret from Charles. She did not tell him that she had practiced a dance routine with former Royal Ballet star Wayne Sleep. On the night of Sleep's performance, she and Charles sat in the royal box at the theater. Diana slipped out of the box during the next to the last number of the program. Then she appeared on stage wearing a silver silk dress, tights, and ballet shoes. She and Sleep danced to the music of "Uptown Girls." The delighted audience demanded eight curtain calls. In public, Charles applauded his wife. In private, he scolded her for being undignified.

Around this time, a story appeared in the newspapers, reviving gossip started six years before. A reporter had discovered the truth about the secret visitor to the royal railroad car, the visitor believed to be Diana. As Diana had insisted, it was not she. The reporter revealed the name of the visitor—Camilla Parker-Bowles.

The couple continued to do some touring together—to Majorca, Oman and Saudi Arabia, Portugal, and Spain. In

Spain, a reporter asked them to explain the fact that they were seldom seen together in their home country. Diana explained: "My husband and I get around two thousand invitations every six months. We can't do them all but if we split them up, with him doing some and me others, we can fulfill twice as many."

Besides a full schedule of official engagements, Diana became interested in AIDS work. She was especially sympathetic to victims of AIDS because of the stigma attached to them. Few people knew much about the disease except that it was deadly, and that it was often carried by sexual contact and illegal drugs. Many incorrectly feared that a person could catch it by simply touching a person infected with the disease. For this reason, few people would care for, or even sympathize with, AIDS patients.

Diana announced that she wanted to visit AIDS patients in a hospital. The royal staff resisted. They did not want Diana to associate with patients who could be homosexuals or drug addicts. Diana produced studies that showed that many AIDS victims had no connection with either homosexuality or drugs. Finally, the palace staff agreed that she could go.

She made sure that photographers caught her shaking hands with patients and hugging them. She wanted to dispel the myth that AIDS was spread through such touching. One of the fundraisers said of Diana's visit to the hospital: "...when the Princess picked up a baby with AIDS ... it took all the stigma out of it [AIDS]." Diana put it in her own words: "HIV does not make people dangerous to know, so you can shake their hands and give them a hug. Heaven knows, they need it."

In April 1987, she opened the first AIDS ward in Britain, in Middlesex Hospital in London. She received hate mail from people who believed that AIDS patients deserve their disease and should not be helped. Still, she continued the work.

She also worked in drug addiction centers. She became a patron of Turning Point, a national charity that helped drug addicts, alcoholics, and mental health patients. She sometimes visited in disguise without police protection. When the royal staff heard of this, they told her she could not do that. They explained that an irrational patient might attack her. Diana refused to stop her visits. Queen Elizabeth invited Diana to tea and told her personally of the dangers she faced. Diana still refused to back down

Besides writing up their formal activities, the press reported that both Charles and Diana had time for some personal life. Stories appeared about Diana going out with an old friend, Major David Waterhouse, and of Charles' continuing affair with Camilla. Often, Camilla substituted for Diana as hostess at Charles' parties. One night, Charles excused his wife's absence saying that she was tired. Everyone knew he had lied when they saw photos of Diana and Waterhouse in the paper the next day.

Charles and Diana went to a wedding together, and Charles left before Diana did. She danced until six the next morning, frequently with twenty-eight-year-old Philip Dunne, a banker. Then Diana and Dunne were spotted together by reporters at sophisticated restaurants. Gossip columns soon linked Diana's name with Dunne's. The gossip increased when Diana chose Dunne to ride with her in a procession that preceded the racing at Royal Ascot.

Another night, photographers spotted Diana and Waterhouse leaving a party. They could not resist Diana's bright red satin trousers and bomber jacket, and they began to take shots of the couple. Diana pleaded with them: "I must have that film—you don't know what this could do to me. I feel so trapped. Please, please..." When the photographers gave her the film, she turned quickly and said good-bye without another word.

Diana and Charles toured Wales together after a massive flood. They gave comfort to the stricken people, but they hardly spoke to each other.

One day Diana left Kensington Palace without informing security that she was leaving. A bodyguard discovered her missing and immediately rushed out to find her. By the time he caught up with her, she was involved in a high-speed chase with a car full of men who had recognized her. She managed to lose them after racing through streets, turning, switching, and changing direction. The security officials insisted that this incident demonstrated the need for twenty-four-hour surveillance of the princess.

Diana was friends with Sarah Ferguson, better known as Fergie, who became duchess of York when she married Prince Andrew, Charles's younger brother. The press also pursued Fergie who, unlike Diana, had a strong sense of self-confidence.

Some of this confidence seemed to rub off on Diana as they enjoyed each other's company. They often went to dinners and parties where they laughed and joked and had the kind of fun Diana remembered from her bachelor girl days.

The two women loved playing tricks. One night they dressed up like policewomen and crashed Prince Andrew's stag party. They didn't fool anyone with their disguises, but the guests at the party enjoyed the joke anyway. Once at Windsor Castle, they did an improvised can-can dance to surprise the guests. On a ski trail in Switzerland, they played around with snowball fights. The press loved the hijinks; the royal family, especially Charles, asked them to stop immediately.

Now it was frequently Charles who was the lonely one of the couple. Diana was not at home very often, and when she was, she frequently entertained her own friends informally. A couple of times Charles joined her with her friends for an evening out. But he complained that they were too young and their activities were immature. This was another basis for arguments between them.

In the fall of 1987, Charles stayed at Balmoral for the month while Diana stayed at Kensington Palace. The newspapers were filled with speculation about the separation and hints about Diana seeing other men and about Charles and Camilla at Balmoral.

Queen Elizabeth invited Charles and Diana to tea at Buckingham Palace. She told them that, no matter what the problems, they could not be divorced. Some of the household staff who served at the tea reported that the queen said it was Charles' responsibility to straighten out the situation because he was more experienced than Diana in royal matters. No one reported on Charles and Diana's reactions.

Diana continued to enjoy nights out, dancing until the early morning and ignoring many of her royal duties. Still, she could not completely ignore royal supervision. She could not simply meet friends at lunch, for example. Even such a personal appointment had to be noted on her daily schedule and announced to all her staff. Scotland Yard was notified of her itinerary. An ambulance squad and fire brigade readied itself near the restaurant. As soon as she started up her blue Jaguar XJS, a royal bodyguard fell into line behind her.

In early 1988, Diana's friend Carolyn discovered that Diana's problem was not merely jangling nerves and stress. She was sure that Diana was dangerously bulimic. Carolyn could not allow her friend to destroy herself. She gave Diana an ultimatum. Either Diana would go to a doctor or Carolyn would call the press and force public attention on the issue.

Diana discussed her problem with her family doctor, a specialist in eating disorders. After a two-hour interview, the doctor promised that she could get rid of her problem in six months. His prescription included admitting that she was a victim of the disease and reading about causes and prevention. Some reports say that Diana came to understand that some of the pain that led to her bulimia was caused by her husband's relationship with Camilla. These reports say that Diana openly accused Camilla of causing trouble in their marriage. They also say that this open accusation helped Diana to feel less consumed by jealousy and resentment.

Charles and Diana found a way to communicate that cut down on arguments. They wrote each other notes about the children, engagements, schedules, and other aspects of their lives. Sometimes they answered the notes personally. At other times they let a staff member handle them.

Diana wanted William to have riding lessons. Charles might have arranged this instead of Diana, who still feared horses because of her fall from her pony many years before. But when Charles did not take care of it, Diana took William to Combermere Barracks for riding lessons. Major James Hewitt, a tank commander during the Gulf War battles, helped with the teaching. Both boys liked and admired Hewitt, and he soon had them riding and enjoying it.

Then Hewitt asked Diana if she would like to try to overcome her fears. She agreed. Hewitt was gentle and patient, and Diana was soon riding on her own. She even grew to like the sport. As the weather turned wet and cold in November, she continued her lessons with Hewitt on the indoor track. Gossip grew about the relationship between Diana and Hewitt. Both tried to ignore it. Finally, the gossip about Hewitt disappeared, its place taken by rumors about Diana and James Gilbey, an automotive dealer. They were often seen leaving and entering restaurants together.

Raine showed up in Diana's life again. When Diana's brother, Charles, was married, Raine snubbed Diana and Charles' mother, Frances. Diana challenged her on this. Raine answered that she snubbed Frances because Frances had inflicted so much pain on Johnnie. Diana answered that Raine did not even know the meaning of pain. "In my role, I see people suffer like you'll never see," she said. "You've got a lot to learn."

That March, Charles and Diana went to the Persian Gulf together. Their mission was to visit British troops stationed there. When Charles vacationed in Turkey a little later, Camilla, not Diana, was with him.

Diana resolved to visit children of the Third World. "I will be going solo on these trips. My husband is too busy with his own organizations," she announced.

She also gave time to Relate, an organization formed to help couples improve their marriages. With her experience as a child of a broken marriage and her trouble with Charles, Diana related easily to the clients. At a lunch for Relate, she said, "I have seen the tears, the anguish, the raw emotions, hurt and pain caused by the split between couples."

As a patron of the British Deaf Association, she studied sign language, using a videotaped lesson. After two weeks, she used some sign language in her speech to the organization.

An official at Dr. Bernado's, Britain's largest child-care institution, said, "The parents of physically handicapped children, who may be dribbling or be a bit of a mess, have a finely tuned instinct for the reaction of other adults. They watch the princess particularly closely. She passes that critical test. The princess accepts these youngsters no matter how bent or buckled they may be." She also worked with Childline, a phone service for abused children.

Earlier, Diana had consulted with an astrologer. She did so again. She used the charts as a method of self-analysis rather than as a guide for daily life. A therapist combined massage with vitamin supplements and a strong belief in the coordination of mind and body as a goal to well-being. She was also interested in Eastern approaches to health like acupuncture, aromatherapy, and tai chi chuan. She joined several different health clubs and worked on aerobics, Nautilus machines, and took dance classes. But each time she joined a club, photographers found her. She had to drop membership at each club to avoid being hounded by them every time she went in and out.

Charles broke his arm playing polo in June 1990. He spent many weeks in hospitals and went through two operations. Diana visited him frequently. While Diana was in the hospital to see Charles, she also visited with many other patients. In talking about Diana, a nurse said: "They [the patients] *were* her. She was just their souls, free for a day, in a beautiful body that walked so straight and breathed so easily. The sick, she would often say, were more real to her than the well: their guard was down, they were themselves." Newspaper reports said that Camilla also visited Charles in the hospital, cut his meat for him, read to him, and in other ways cared for him.

When Charles no longer needed hospital care, he recuperated at Balmoral and Highgrove. Rumors said that Camilla often visited him during this time. Sometimes Diana brought the boys

Diana's visits with AIDS patients helped calm fears about the new and frightening disease.

from Kensington to Highgrove to visit. A member of the household staff said that Charles and Diana had very little contact with each other at these times. Charles often worked in his vegetable garden. He tried to get the boys interested in his garden, but they preferred riding and other sports. For her part, Diana often stayed in her sitting room. She enjoyed reading. Danielle Steel was one of her favorite romantic authors; Kahlil Gibran was a favorite philosopher.

They shared family meals, but the couple chatted mostly with the boys, not with each other. When they did talk to each other, they often ended up in loud arguments that were never resolved.

In December 1990, Diana broke another royal rule. She spoke against the government's plan of getting rid of mental institutions by returning former inmates to their community. Diana said that those who advocated the plan did not understand the reality of the world faced by patients with mental problems.

In the winter of 1990-1991, she made seven visits to shelters for the homeless. Some met her with aggressive questions comparing her living situation with theirs. She listened attentively. She appeared to be comfortable in all situations.

When Barbara Bush, wife of President George Bush, visited in London, Diana took her to Middlesex Hospital to visit AIDS patients. One patient asked Diana why she spent time with suffering people. She answered, "Anywhere I see suffering, that is where I want to be, doing what I can."

She also visited Broadmoor, a maximum-security prison. She talked with some inmates in groups and with some in their cells. "Living with the royal family is an ideal preparation for going to Broadmoor," she joked.

She was a royal patron of seventy charities, and often began work at six in the morning and kept pushing until the end of an evening function. On a typical day, Diana visited the local Relate center in the morning to talk with staff and couples for two hours. Then she talked to members of the Women's Survivor's Group, an organization which helps women who were abused as children. Then she launched a $20-million appeal for the Foundation for Conductive Education, a center to care for victims of cerebral palsy, especially children. She went on to Drugline, an organization that received seven distress calls a month from drug addicts. There she spoke with both clinic staff and addicts. She arrived home about seven that night, just in time to read a story to Harry.

Chapter Seven

"Whatever happens, I will always love you.
—Charles to Camilla

On Diana's thirtieth birthday in 1991, a national poll declared that she was the most popular member of the royal family. The front page of the *Daily Mail* shouted out a story that Diana had refused her husband's offer of a birthday party. She countered that she thought a party would be frivolous at a time when British troops were fighting in the Gulf War. Diana celebrated her birthday quietly with her children and Jane.

William was accidentally hit by a golf club at school. Doctors diagnosed a depressed fracture of the skull. They said they would have to operate immediately to see if they could remove pressure on the brain caused by a small piece of bone that was forced inward. They had no way to know if the brain was already damaged, and they could give no guarantee about the success of the surgery. Charles and Diana waited together through the seventy-five-minute operation. The doctors came out of surgery saying that William would suffer no permanent damage.

Charles then left for an overnight trip to Yorkshire to attend a study of the environment. Diana stayed with her son, holding his hand, and watching as nurses came in every twenty minutes to check blood pressure and reflexes. She refused to leave William's side. When Charles returned to the hospital, he accused her of being over-protective.

Diana broke another royal tradition that December. She sent out Christmas cards signed "Lots of love, Diana." Until that year, members of the royal family always sent out cards signed by both members of the couple. Diana said that she could not be tied to royal regulations since she had never been taught them. "Just nobody helped me at all," she said of the royal family and staff. Britons were shocked. They believed that Elizabeth, the Queen Mother, and others had given Diana a lot of information and advice on her new role even before she married Charles.

In her traditional Christmas message that year, Elizabeth II announced that she expected to serve the nation for years to come. Reports said that this enraged Charles, who hoped that his mother would abdicate in favor of him, perhaps in the near future. Many people thought that Elizabeth refused to abdicate since it meant that Diana would become queen.

Charles and Diana made an official six-day tour of India. After a polo match, Diana presented prizes to the players. When she gave a prize to Charles, he tried to kiss her on the cheek. She turned her face away, and a hundred photographers snapped a picture of the rejection.

Diana visited the hospice at Mother Teresa's mission in Calcutta. She sat by beds of incurable patients, giving them the comfort of her presence and helping physically where possible.

When Prince William was struck by a golf club and severely wounded, Diana sat by his bed for days.

Soon after, she flew to Rome to see Mother Teresa, who was ill. They prayed together, perhaps strengthening Diana's resolve to concentrate on those less fortunate then she was.

Diana broke another strong royal tradition. Members of the royal family always bought British cars—Charles drove a Bentley Turbo and an Aston-Martin. Diana leased a bright red open-topped Mercedes-Benz 500SL.

In March 1992, Diana's sixty-eight-year-old father died from pneumonia. Diana and Charles attended the funeral together. Diana sent a wreath with a card: "I miss you dreadfully Darling Daddy, but will love you forever. Diana."

That June, author Andrew Morton, a leading authority on royal family and tradition, published a book, *Diana, Her True Story*. He explained that Diana had not spoken to him personally, but she had given her friends permission to tell him anything they wanted to. She admitted that the book would create problems for the royal family, but she said, "I was just so fed up with being seen as a basket case. I thought there might be a better understanding of me." In the book, Diana is quoted as telling a friend: "The night before the wedding I was very calm, deathly calm. I felt I was the lamb to the slaughter." Another quote is Charles telling Camilla, "Whatever happens I will always love you." Another passage quotes Diana's answer to a doctor's question about how many times she tried to commit suicide—"Four or five times." The book hit Britain and the whole world with a storm of controversy. The *Sunday Times* printed excerpts.

Queen Elizabeth tried to deflect the criticism of the royal family and of Prince Charles in the book. She and the royal staff instigated a public relations program to show Charles as devoted to his people and to his career. One staff report suggested that the marriage might be saved if Diana would agree to go for counseling.

In July, Diana and Charles discussed separation. They each had lawyers advising them.

In August came revelations even more startling than those in Morton's book. Transcripts of taped conversations between Diana and James Gilbey, recorded in 1989, appeared in the *The Sun*. They were called the Squidgy tapes because that was the nickname that Gilbey used for Diana. In the conversations, both Diana and Gilbey spoke of their strong love and their physical and emotional need for each other.

Immediately, the staff at Buckingham Palace denounced the tapes as fakes. Then they said they weren't sure. Then the rumor went around that Elizabeth was studying the question of divorce and Charles' ascension to the throne with lawyers.

At first, people questioned the validity of the tapes, believing that such taping was difficult to do. But royal surveillance is strongly organized. It is believed that six men pursue a round-the-clock surveillance of all calls that pass through the royal switchboards. The tapes are sent to a government center where they are reviewed. Material considered sensitive is sent on to government officials. Some is retained in security files. Some is destroyed.

Diana's visits with Mother Teresa strengthened her conviction to help the poor.

The couple was nicknamed the Glums in November 1992 when they made a tour of South Korea together. Less and less frequently they pretended to get along. Each performed the necessary royal duty, and this did not include showing affection for each other.

In an agreement with each other and with Elizabeth and Philip, the young couple did some negotiating. Neither wanted to cite adultery or cruelty as a cause for divorce. So they planned a two-year separation, which was a legal requirement for a divorce which did not cite these causes.

Diana would lead a separate life in the royal framework, appearing with Charles only on formal occasions. Charles would move out of Kensington Palace.

In December 1992, Prime Minister John Major addressed the House of Commons: "It is announced from Buckingham Palace that, with regret, the Prince and Princess of Wales have decided to separate." When asked about the announcement, Diana said, "...my husband asked for the separation and I supported it."

In January 1993, *The Daily Mirror* printed another set of tapes of phone conversations. These were between Charles and Camilla and contained many references to their sexual desire for each other.

Diana's questions about her future revolved around her children and her role in life. After a divorce, would she lose the children? Would she be able to work as effectively with her charity projects if she were not a princess?

Charles' questions concerned his ascension to the throne.

Would the Church of England allow him to become king? Would public pressure prevent him from marrying again if he wanted to?

In 1993 Diana asked for an appointment with Prime Minister Majors. She talked to him about becoming a roving ambassador for Britain. She said that she believed some of the conflicts in the world were continued because pride, especially male pride, stalled communication. Diana said that she would use a more sensitive intuitive approach. Majors was enthusiastic.

But when he suggested the appointment to Buckingham Palace, he ran into a stone wall. The royal staff believed that the role Diana described was perfect for Charles. Diana was annoyed that the prime minister had bothered with the formality of asking for royal approval. The royal staff was indignant that Diana had spoken to the prime minister before consulting them.

She ran into another royal roadblock when she expressed sympathy to families whose children had been killed in a terrorist attack. She told them she wanted to be at the funeral. But Buckingham Palace had already publicly decided that Prince Philip would be the representative of the crown.

Diana decided that she needed to become a more polished public speaker. In September 1993, she had her first voice coaching lessons with Peter Settelen, a former star of a TV soap drama. Settleten helped her with breathing and articulation and also helped her to write some speeches.

Some critics said that her speeches were full of amateur psychology and worthless phrases. Dismayed at these reports, she looked at the rest of her activities. She decided that her personal visits to places like hospices and homes for battered women were no longer satisfying to her. She believed that she might be turning into an automaton, smiling and shaking hands, but with little depth or insight into the situations she was facing.

Diana once again fell into despair, sleeplessness, and bouts of weeping. Her temper was short. Once she jabbed a reporter in the chest and yelled, "You make my life hell." She hoped that a vacation would help. But photographers hounded her and the boys in a tour of Disney World, and she arrived back in London more depressed than ever.

Then a series of unfortunate press incidents hit Diana one after another. A photographer from the magazine *Hello!* claimed to have photos of Diana sunbathing topless in a Spanish hotel. Diana denied that she had been doing so. The hotel where Diana had been staying bought the photos anyway, to avoid the potential problem. The story appeared in the papers without the photos. When she met with a reporter friend from the *Daily Mail,* somebody snapped photos of the meeting. And the supposed friend wrote an article on their conversation that she had considered private.

Diana worked out regularly in a health club. She was enraged when she saw photos of herself on a leg press, photos snapped by a camera hidden in the ceiling of the club. She went to court to sue for invasion of privacy. The defendants argued that she didn't object to photos snapped of her visiting AIDS patients or children. They said that she had no right to allow photography in some places and not in others. The case was never brought to trial. A confidential agreement was reached between the two parties.

In December 1993, Diana gave a speech after a charity luncheon to raise money for the National Head Injuries Association. The queen and the prime minister had agreed to the content of the speech. She opened her five-minute speech: "When I started my public life twelve years ago, I understood that the media might be interested in what I did." She went on to say that she was going to rebuild her private life with a focus on her two sons and a decrease in her charity work. After the speech, Diana was exhausted with the emotion of it, but also exhilarated. She had said what she wanted to say in her own words. And she had broken a little more tradition by making the announcement herself instead of having it made through Buckingham Palace.

More trouble came with a story in *The Daily Express* in March. James Hewitt told intimate details about his relationship with Diana.

In the spring of 1994, Diana made a visit to America. She made many friends there, including Katharine Graham, then editor of the *Washington Post*. She told Graham, "I want them [my sons] to grow up knowing there are poor people as well as palaces." The two women had many conversations. Another comment that Graham remembers came in answer to Graham's question if Diana would like to go to college. Diana answered readily, "I've already had an education." She also told Graham that she wanted to work only in areas where she could expect to make a difference in people's lives. In Harlem, New York, she visited a children's AIDS center and also toured a hostel for the homeless.

In June, Charles admitted in a television interview that he had been unfaithful. Over 13.5 million people watched the show; Diana did not. He was evasive when asked about the possibility of divorce, saying only that it was not a matter to be discussed at that time. He was not evasive about his future role as king and head of the church. He said he wanted to be Defender of Faith, not Defender of *the* Faith. The first Diana heard of Charles' confession was the headline that screamed the news of Charles' infidelity. She rushed to her sons' school to explain to them that their mother and father did not love each other any more, but they both dearly loved their sons.

In June 1994, author Jonathan Dimbleby published an authorized biography of Charles, *Prince of Wales: A Biography*. In the book, Charles said that he had never loved Diana. He had married her only because of pressure from his family. This statement brought strong support for Diana from many citizens who were angry that she had been betrayed as far back as the engagement.

Next came the story of three hundred phone calls to a private home where the caller hung up as soon as someone answered. These calls were traced to Diana's phones, to her sister's phone, and to public telephones near Kensington Palace. Diana insisted that she had not made the calls and did not know who did.

Reporters pondered the question: Is the royal family out to "get" Diana?

In October, the book *Princess in Love* was published. This book, authorized by Hewitt, told of his five-year affair with Diana. It included stories about Hewitt staying over at Kensington Palace when Charles was away.

The end of the two-year separation, December 1994, was fast approaching. One important question was about the children: Diana wanted all the time and influence she could get. Another question was about finances. Technically, Charles was not a rich man. Most of "his" money was tied up in trusts, locked away for his heirs. If Diana were to get a settlement of any size, it would have to come from Queen Elizabeth's money. Diana's lawyers urged her not to hurry to make any decision. They said Diana's position would be stronger if the royal family approached her first. Publicly Diana insisted, "Our boys, that's all that matters." As partial explanation of what had happened to her marriage, she blamed Charles for not accepting changes in her: "I've always been the eighteen-year-old girl he got engaged to, so I don't think I've been given any credit for growth."

Diana tried to bury her thoughts in her work, setting up day-long visits to hospices where she assisted in nursing care. She did everything from emptying bedpans to running errands. She was also close when friends and family needed comfort—the widow of a well-known politician, the mother of an infant who died at eleven months, the parents of a baby who was kidnapped.

She liked to bring her sons with her when she went to help people. Once, she took the princes to a shelter for homeless people. While there, Diana talked with the people, and William and Harry played chess and cards with them.

In November 1995, Diana took part in a fifty-five-minute interview on BBC watched by over twenty-one million British viewers. The interviewer was correspondent Martin Bashir. She told of her fears on becoming a royal figure: "I was very daunted because as far as I was concerned I was a fat, chubby twenty-one-year-old." She said about her marriage: "I desperately loved my husband, and I wanted to share everything, and I thought we were a good team." When asked about Camilla, she said, "...there were three of us in this marriage ...so it was a bit crowded." She also admitted that she had been in love with Hewitt. She spoke openly of her problems with bulimia and self-inflicted pain. She said she would take half of the responsibility for problems in the marriage, but it would be Charles who would make the ultimate decision of whether to divorce.

A week after the broadcast, eighty-three percent of the viewers said they liked her more because of the interview. A few months later, she topped the list of popular persons in the British opinion polls. She received three times the ratings of Queen Elizabeth and seven times those of Charles.

In February 1996, Diana announced that she had agreed to a divorce. Her spokeswoman said that Diana would remain involved in all decisions about the children, that she would

In November 1995, Diana gave a fifty-five minute interview to the BBC.

remain at Kensington Palace, and that she would retain the title Princess of Wales. The royal staff immediately denied that any such decisions had been made.

A few days later, Diana called the *Daily Mail* to tell a reporter that the palace was "playing Ping-Pong with me... I have given them everything they wanted, and they are still not satisfied." Diana's lawyer sent a letter to Charles saying that the divorce would be called off if Charles did not meet Diana's demands.

On August 28, 1996, Diana and Charles' divorce became final. Under the agreement, she received a lump sum payment of $26.5 million plus $600,000 a year to maintain her office and bedroom apartment in Kensington Palace. She and Charles would share custody of their sons. They would spend half their vacations with their father and half with their mother. Diana no longer had the title "Her Royal Highness."

Diana concentrated on the causes she cared most about. AIDS and cancer victims were at the top of her list. When a reporter asked if she could continue with her volunteer work with the same strength she had as a princess, she had a ready answer. "I've been in a privileged position for fifteen years," she replied, "and I've got tremendous knowledge about people and how to communicate—I've learned that, I've got that. And I want to use it."

In the fall of 1996, she made another visit to America where she was again greeted by cheering crowds. First Lady Hillary Rodham Clinton threw a gala party for her. She also visited AIDS children in Washington, D.C. When a three-year-old victim asked for a ride in her car, Diana agreed with a smile. Diana was presented the prestigious Humanitarian Award at the 41st Annual United Cerebral Palsy Awards Dinner in New York.

On that tour, she lunched with Tina Brown, editor of *The New Yorker* and Anna Wintour, editor of *Vogue*. Diana told her friends that she believed the royalty was in serious need of help with public relations. "They kept saying I was manipulative. But what's the alternative? To just sit there and have them make your image for you?" She spoke of her son, "But William—I think he has it. I think he understands." She regretted that she could not be queen. "We would have been the best team in the world. I could shake hands till the cows come home. And Charles could make serious speeches."

At an auction, Diana's gowns were sold for charities. One gown brought over $100,000; the total earned was $3.26 million. The money benefited a number of charities, including Sloan-Kettering Cancer Cancer and the AIDS Care Center of Cornell Medical Center. Mother Teresa posed for photographs with her on the steps of a charity in the South Bronx in New York.

Chapter Eight

"She was the people's princess."
—Prime Minister Tony Blair to the world

In the early summer of 1997, Diana began dating a man whom she had met about ten years before. Forty-one-year-old Emad "Dodi" Fayed was the son of one of the wealthiest men in the world. He was a businessman with interests in many ventures, including the American movies *Chariots of Fire*, *F/X*, *Hook*, and *The Scarlet Letter*. The Fayed family made a sharp contrast to Charles' family. They were emotionally warm and open, and they did not follow a strict code of behavior and dress.

In early July, Diana and her sons vacationed on one of Dodi's yachts near St. Tropez on the French Riviera. The press hovered in helicopters, planes, and boats. Diana complained to a photographer that the cameras bothered the boys. This did not stop the photographers.

Later that month, Diana and Dodi again enjoyed a vacation alone on his yacht. A photographer used a long lens to snap a picture of Dodi and Diana in an embrace. The photo was immediately named "The Kiss" and may have earned the photographer three-quarters of a million dollars.

In August, Diana made a tour to Bosnia, a war-torn country on the Adriatic Sea. She was keeping a promise to study the damage caused by land mines, explosive devices that are set off when a person steps on them. Land mines are so delicate that even a child's step can cause an explosion. She visited a shantytown in Sarajevo. There she spoke with victims of land mines—children who had lost limbs and grieving relatives of those killed. She enraged the monarchy by criticizing Britain's policy of planting land mines.

Later in August, Diana and Dodi met for a vacation on the Cote d'Azur of the Riviera. Photographers swarmed over them. Photographers also showed up on their vacation in Sardinia, an island in the Mediterranean Sea.

After that trip, Diana planned to return to London to see her sons. They would have finished their month-long visit with Charles. In Paris, she told reporters: "... any sane person would have left [Britain] long ago. But I cannot. I have my sons."

On their last night together before Diana would fly to England, she and Dodi dined in a private salon at the Ritz, a fashionable restaurant owned by Dodi's father. The press waited for her. A few minutes after midnight, Diana and Dodi slipped out a back door into the hotel's waiting Mercedes S-600. A hotel security man drove; a bodyguard rode beside him. Dodi and Diana sat in the back seat. Probably they were headed for Dodi's father's town house, about four miles away. With photographers chasing, the driver sped past the fountains and obelisk of the Place de la Concorde.

They raced into a narrow tunnel across the Seine from the Eiffel Tower. A motorcycle, a motor scooter, and at least one car chased them. Just after the Mercedes entered the tunnel, the driver lost control. The car continued into the tunnel, striking a pillar on the side. It ricocheted off the opposite wall. The front of the sedan folded into the front seat. The roof collapsed.

The photographers arrived on the scene. One of them used his cell phone to call emergency services. It was reported that other photographers pressed against the car windows to take shots of Diana.

Ten minutes later, an ambulance arrived. Dodi and the driver were pronounced dead. The bodyguard, Rees-Jones, was taken to the hospital. The crew worked an hour to free Diana from the wreckage. They rushed her to a hospital four miles away, where she was immediately wheeled into emergency surgery. She did not regain consciousness after the accident. The medical team found severe head injuries, major damage to her left lung, and profuse bleeding from her chest cavity. After two hours of internal and external heart massage, the medical team pronounced her dead of cardiac arrest. It was 4 a.m. on August 31, 1997. The death notice was delayed two hours so that Prince Charles could be the first to tell their children what had happened. Then Charles flew to Paris with Diana's sisters to return the princess' body to England.

British Prime Minister Tony Blair told the world about the tragedy: "She was the people's princess, and that is how she will stay in our hearts and memories forever."

News reports focused on her death and then on the fact that her driver had been chased by photographers. Questions arose: Was the driver really going over 120 miles an hour? Was her driver drunk at the time of the accident? Should the photographers be blamed because they encouraged the driver to speed? Were any photographers guilty of breaking the French law that says a person who has seen an accident must offer help to the injured? The police held seven photographers. Diana's brother, the ninth Earl Spencer, said that, "every editor of every publication that has paid for intrusive and exploitive photographs of her . . . has her blood on their hands."

The only survivor, Rees-Jones the security guard, lay in a hospital in critical condition and unable to speak.

News of her death spread around the world. People sobbed in the streets, stores, and homes all over England and the world. Charles, William and Harry, Queen Elizabeth and the Queen Mother remained in seclusion in Balmoral. A public cry went out for expressions of mourning from the royal family. An editorial in *The Sun* said: "...not one tear has been shed in public from a royal eye. It is as if no one in the royal family has a soul." Four days after the tragedy, the queen's press secretary said, "the royal family have been hurt by suggestions that they are indifferent to the country's sorrow." That evening, the royal family went outside the gates of Balmoral to look over tributes to Diana. The press watched, took photographs, and approved.

Except for an annual Christmas message, Queen Elizabeth had addressed her people on television only once before. That

Prince William and Prince Henry await the beginning of Dianar's funeral procession.

time she had spoken about the Gulf War. Now she spoke again on TV. Part of what she said was "I want to pay tribute to Diana myself. She was an exceptional and gifted human being."

The funeral procession route was extended several times during the week as the estimates of attendance were increased several times. Prime Minister Tony Blair proclaimed the day of the funeral a national day of mourning. Huge screens were set up in Hyde Park so that people could watch the ceremony over closed circuit television. Millions lined the streets.

The procession began at Kensington Palace. At St. James's Palace, Prince Charles, William and Harry, Prince Philip, and Diana's brother joined the cortege. They walked a few paces behind the carriage that carried the coffin. After them came representatives of charities Diana had supported: AIDS victims, homeless people,Red Cross representatives, and victims of land mines. Some were on crutches and in wheelchairs.

Charles Spencer demanded that no tabloid editor be allowed to attend. Acres of flowers lined the funeral route from the Spencer estate to Westminster Abbey.

At Westminster Abbey, Welsh Guards in crimson uniforms raised the casket to their shoulders. They took it down the long aisle of the church and placed it at the front of the altar. After laying a bouquet of white lilies at the foot of the coffin, Prince Charles and Prince Philip led William and Harry, Queen Elizabeth II, and the Queen Mother to seats in the front of the sanctuary. About two thousand mourners were seated behind them. Her brother Charles said, "Above all, we give thanks for the life of a woman I am so proud to be able to call my sister; the unique, the complex, the extraordinary and irreplaceable Diana, whose beauty, both internal and external, will never be extinguished from our minds." The dean of Westminster said, "Diana profoundly influenced this nation and the world." At William's suggestion, Elton John sang "Candle in the Wind," in which he made specific reference to Diana: "Your footsteps will always fall here/among England's greenest hills;/your candle's burned out long before/your legend ever will."

The funeral procession made a two-hour trip to the Spencer family home. Along the way, crowds sobbed and threw flowers.

Diana was buried on an island in the middle of a small lake on the family estate. The burial was private.

Afterword

In September 1997, Andrew Morton published another book about Diana. He said that this book contained the facts behind his 1992 book *Diana: Her True Story*. He said that he and Diana had not told the whole truth about that book when they said that he had not discussed the book with her. In his new book, Morton claims that Diana had talked with him personally and at length while he was writing *Diana: Her True Story*. But she made Morton promise not to tell because she believed that this revelation would be too difficult for the royal family. However, now that she was dead, Morton said he had the duty to get Diana's message out to the public. He had tapes of Diana's conversations with him, and he issued a revision of the book, using some of these tapes. This book is titled *Diana: Her True Story in Her Own Words*.

Also in September, Trevor Rees-Jones, a bodyguard in the car in which Diana was killed, recovered enough to recuperate at home. According to police, he could offer no important information to the report of the accident. It is suspected that his head injuries and shock blotted out his memory of the tragedy.

A judge ordered toxicology tests on the body of Henri Paul,

the driver of the car. His blood alcohol level was 1.75 grams per liter of blood, three times above the level considered legally drunk by French law.

Crash witnesses reported that they saw a white car speeding away after the accident. The car, possibly a Fiat Uno, may have grazed the Mercedes just before the crash. An extensive search for the car yielded no results.

In December, Trevor Rees-Jones, after recovering at home, was interviewed by a judge. Rees-Jones, his face badly scarred, walked with an unsteady step. He said that he did not recall any details of the accident.

Then, in March of 1998, Rees-Jones said he now remembered some details of the accident. With the help of psychiatrists trained in post-accident trauma, Rees-Jones related some of the details to French investigators. He was quoted as saying that Diana was conscious immediately after the crash and that she did speak at that time. He remembered her calling out Dodi's name. He also said that Henri Paul did not seem drunk that evening. Investigators delayed a full report while questioning continued.

Also in March, Diana's will was made public by her family lawyers. Her mother was named an executor of the estate that totaled about $35.6 million. Diana left the bulk of this in trust to her sons Prince William and Prince Harry.

Titles of the British Nobility

_____

_____

Baron, Baroness

Originally, the term baron signified a person who owned land as a direct gift from the monarchy or as a descendent of a baron. Now it is an honorary title. The wife of a baron is a baroness.

Duke, Duchess, Duchy, Dukedom

Originally, a man could become a duke in one of two ways. He could be recognized for owning a lot of land. Or he could be a victorious military commander. Now a man can become a duke simply by being appointed by a monarch. Queen Elizabeth II appointed her husband Philip the Duke of Edinburgh and her son Charles the Duke of Wales. A duchess is the wife or widow of a duke. The territory ruled by a duke is a duchy or a dukedom.

Earl, Earldom

Earl is the oldest title in the English nobility. It originally signified a chieftan or leader of a tribe. Each earl is identified with a certain area called an earldom. Today the monarchy sometimes confers an earldom on a retiring prime minister. For example, former Prime Minister Harold Macmillan is the Earl of Stockton

King

A king is a ruling monarch. He inherits this position and retains it until he abdicates or dies. Formerly, a king was an absolute ruler. Today the role of King of England is largely symbolic. The wife of a king is a queen.

Knight

Originally a knight was a man who performed devoted military service. The title is not hereditary. A king or queen may award a citizen with knighthood. The criterion for the award is devoted service to the country.

Lady

One may use Lady to refer to the wife of a knight, baron, count, or viscount. It may also be used for the daughter of a duke, marquis, or earl. **Marquis,** also spelled **Marquess.** A marquis ranks above an earl and below a duke. Originally marquis signified military men who stood guard on the border of a territory. Now it is a hereditary title.

Lord

Lord in a general term denoting nobility. It may be used to address any peer (see below) except a duke. The House of Lords is the upper house of the British Parliament. It is a nonelective body with limited powers. The presiding officer fo the House of Lords is the Lord Chancellor or Lord High Chancellor. Sometimes a mayor is called lord, such as the Lord Mayor of London. The term lord may also be used informally to show respect.

Peer, Peerage

A peer is a titled member of the British nobility who may sit in the House of Lords, the upper house of Parliament. Peers are ranked in order of their importance. A duke is most important; the others follow in this order: marquis, earl, viscount, baron. A group of peers is called a peerage.

Prince, Princess
Princes and princesses are sons and daughters of a reigning king and queen. The first-born son of a royal family is first in line for the throne, the second born son is second in line. A princess may become a queen if there is no prince at the time of abdication or death of the king. The wife of a prince is also called a princess.

Queen
A queen may be the ruler of a monarchy, the wife—or widow—of a king.

Viscount, Viscountess
The title Viscount originally meant deputy to a count. It has been used most recently to honor British soldiers in World War II. Field Marshall Bernard Montgomery was named a viscount. The title may also be hereditary. The wife of a viscount is a viscountess. (In pronunciation the initial *s* is silent.)

House of Windsor
The British royal family has been called the House of Windsor since 1917. Before then, the royal family name was Wettin, a German name derived from Queen Victoria's husband. In 1917, England was at war with Germany. King George V announced that the royal family name would become the House of Windsor, a name derived from Windsor Castle, a royal residence. The House of Windsor has included Kings George V, Edward VIII, George VI, and Queen Elizabeth II.

Bibliography

Buskin, Richard. *Princess Diana: Her Life Story, 1961-1997*. Illinois: Publications International, Ltd., 1997.

Davies, Nicholas. *Diana: A Princess and Her Troubled Marriage*. New York, Carol Publishing Group, 1992.

Dimbleby, Jonathan. *The Prince of Wales: A Biography. New York: William Morrow and Co., Inc., 1994.*

Junor, Penny. *Charles*. New York: St. Martin's Press, 1987.

Junor, Penny. *Diana: Princess of Wales*. New York: Doubleday & Company, 1983.

Lacey, Robert. *Princess*. London: Times Books, 1982.

Martin, Ralph. *Charles & Diana*. New York: G.P. Putnam's Sons, 1985.

Morton, Andrew. *Diana: Her New Life*. New York: Simon & Schuster, Inc., 1995.

Morton, Andrew. *Diana: Her True Story*. New York: Pocket Books, 1992.

Morton, Andrew. *Diana's Diary*. New York: Summit Books, 1990.

The New Yorker, Sept. 15, 1997.

Newsweek, Sept. 8, 1997, Sept. 15, 1997, October 13, 1997.

Perry, George. *Diana: A Celebration*. New York: WHS Publishers, Inc., 1982.

Spoto, Donald. *The Decline and Fall of the House of Windsor*, New York: Pocket Books, 1995.

Time, Sept. 8, 1997, Sept. 15, 1997.

A Tribute to Princess Diana. New York: Biograph Communications, Inc., 1997.

Whitaker, James. *Diana vs Charles: Royal Blood Feud*. New York: A Dutton Book, 1993.

Sources

CHAPTER ONE

p. 9 "she could be obstinate ..." Whitaker, James. *Diana vs Charles: Royal Blood Feud*. New York: Penguin Books USA Inc., 1993. p.97.

p. 10 "She has always loved ..." Martin, Ralph. *Charles & Diana*. New York: G.P.Putnam's Sons, 1985, p.35.

p. 11 "Diana could not be called ..." Whitaker,.op.cit., p.97.

p. 12 "My parents were busy ..." Morton, Andrew. *Diana: Her True Story*. New York: Pocket Books, 1992, p.25.

p. 14 "I'll never ever marry ..." Davies, Nicholas. *Diana: A Princess and Her Troubled Marriage*. New York: Carol Publishing Group, 1992, p.311.

p. 17 "...she was awfully sweet ..." Martin, op.cit., p.40.

p. 17 "It always released tremendous tension." Morton, op.cit., p.39.

p. 18 "someone with whom you could never ..." Martin, op.cit., p.44

p. 19 "Raine, Raine, go away." Davies, op.cit., p.47

p. 20 "I became a great expert ..." Davies, op.cit., p.48

CHAPTER TWO

p. 22 "You should be with someone ..." Morton, op.cit., p.69.

p. 23 "Please, God, may I have ..." Martin, op.cit., p.269

p. 23 "In such circumstances ..." Whitaker, op.cit., p.101

p. 24 "You looked so sad ..." Morton, op.cit., p.69

p. 28 "I have never been on that train." Whitaker, op.cit., p.10

p. 28 "May I ask the editors of Fleet Street ..." Buskin, Richard. *Princess Diana: Her Life Story, 1961-1997*. Illinois: Publications International, Ltd., 1997, p.120.

p. 28 "I really don't know." Martin, op.cit., p.152.

p. 30 "I wanted to photograph ..." Martin. op.cit., p.164.

p. 30 "What will make the marriage ..." Lacey, Robert. *Princess*. London: Times Books, 1982, p.19.

p. 30 "She's got a strong personality ..." Martin, op.cit., p.165.

p. 30 "For God's sake, ring me up." Morton, op.cit., p.84.

p. 32 "Nobody can seriously pretend ..." Spoto, Donald. *The Decline and Fall of the House of Windsor*. New York: Pocket Books, 1995, p.376.

p. 33 "I think she would drop ..." Martin, op.cit., p.195

p. 34 "I wish I could believe ..." Davies, op.cit., p.225

p. 34 "Whatever 'in love' means." *Newsweek*, Sept. 8, 1997, p.43

p. 34 "Diana seemed bowled over ..." Davies, op.cit., p.105.

CHAPTER THREE

p. 35 "I'll be there at the altar ..." Morton, op.cit., 92.

p. 35 "Do you want to feel ..." Lacey, op.cit., p.23.

p. 35 "She wasn't happy ..." Morton, op.cit., p.85.

p. 35 "...if there's going to be a dominant ..." Martin, op.cit., p.204.

p. 36 "We want to make her look ..." Martin. op.cit., p.191.

p. 37 "I'm so proud of you." Morton, op.cit., p.92

p. 40 "You look wonderful." Martin, op.cit., p.215.

p. 40 "Dearly beloved ..." Lacey, op.cit., p.26.

p. 40 "Love is patient, love is..." Bible, Corinthians 13.

p. 43 "speaks it like an angel ..." Lacey, op.cit., p.113

CHAPTER FOUR

p. 44 "I feel totally out of place ..." Davies, op.cit., p.126

p. 44 "I don't need you ..." Davies, op.cit., p.132.

p. 44 "I feel totally out of place..." Davies, op.cit., p.126.

p. 46 "...looking for other ways ..." Martin, op.cit., 271.

p. 46 "Oliver must go." Davies, op.cit., p.155.

p. 47 "that miserable lump." Martin, op.cit, 282.

p. 47 "Interesting condition." Ibid.

p. 48 "Can't he [Charles] understand ..." Davies, op.cit., p.130.

p. 49 "I hate all this heel-clicking." Martin, op.cit., 248.

p. 54 "I'm sorry he's not ..." Martin, op.cit., p.306.

CHAPTER FIVE

p. 55 "The Royal Family is never ..."Martin, op.cit., p.311

p. 55 "Children cannot be left ..." Whitaker, op.cit., 132

p. 56 "I have come to the conclusion ..." Whitaker, op.cit., p.130

p. 56 "Well, the Royal Family ..." Martin, op.cit., p.311

p. 56 "Now I'm going to blow ..." Martin, op.cit., p.312

p. 57"like a spoilt brat." Martin, op.cit., p.314.

p. 57 "Diana eighty percent certain ..." Martin, op.cit., p.313.

p. 60 "mince 'n mash mush." Martin, op.cit., p.345.

p. 61 "The Princess has helped enormously." Davies, op.cit., p.271

p. 62 "Not all that long ago ..." Martin, op.cit., 381

p. 65 "Domo arigato ..." *The New Yorker*, Sept. 15, 1997, p.57.

CHAPTER SIX

p. 66 "Anywhere I see suffering, ..." Buskin, op.cit., p.163.

p. 67 "My husband and I get around ..." Whitaker, op.cit., p.151

p. 67 "When the Princess picked up ..." Davies, op.cit., p.262.

p. 67 "HIV does not make people ..." Davies, op.cit., p.263.

p. 69 "I must have that film." Davies, op.cit., p.205

p. 73 "In my role, I see people suffer ..." Morton, op.cit., p.44.

p. 73 "I will be going solo." Whitaker, op.cit., p.159.

p. 73 "I have seen the tears ..." Whitaker, op.cit., p.160.

p. 73 "The parents of physically handicapped ..." Morton, Andrew. *Diana's Diary*. New York: Summit Books, 1990, p.94.

p. 74 "They [the patients] were her ..." *The New Yorker*, Sept. 15, 1997, p.54.

p. 76 "Anywhere I see suffering ..." Buskin, op.cit., p.163.

p. 77 "Living with the royal family ..." Morton, Andrew. *Diana: Her New Life*. New York: Simon & Schuster, Inc., 1995, p.180.

CHAPTER SEVEN

p. 78 "Whatever happens, I will always ..." Morton, Andrew. *Diana: Her True Story*. New York: Pocket Books, 1992, p.115.

p. 79 "Lots of love, Diana." Davies, op.cit., p.9.

p. 79 "Just nobody helped." Whitaker, op.cit., p.118

p. 81 "I miss you dreadfully ..." Whitaker, op.cit., p.189.

p. 81 "I was just so fed up ..." *A Tribute to Princess Diana*, Biograph Communications, Inc., 1997, p.17.

p. 81 "The night before the wedding ..." Morton, Andrew. *Diana: Her True Story*. op.cit. p.93.

p. 81 "Whatever happens, I will ..." Morton, Andrew. *Diana: Her True Story. op.cit.*, 115.

p. 81 "Four or five times." Morton, Andrew. *Diana: Her True Story*. op.cit., p.147.

p. 84 "It is announced from Buckingham Palace ..." Whitaker, op.cit., p174.

p. 84 "My husband asked for the separation ..." *A Tribute to Princess Diana*, op.cit., p.19.

p. 86 "You make my life hell." http://www.pbs.org

p. 87 "When I started my public life ..." Morton, Andrew. *Diana: Her New Life*, op.cit., p.138-9.

p. 87 "I want them [my sons] to ..." Newsweek, Sept. 15, 1997, p.68.

p. 87 "I've already had an education." Ibid.

p. 89 "Our boys, that's all that matters." *A Tribute to Princess Diana*, op.cit., p.56

p. 89 "I've always been the 18-year-old." http://www.pbs.org.

p. 90 "I was very daunted because ..." Ibid.

p. 90 "I desperately loved my husband ..." *Time*, Sept. 15, 1997, p.97.

p. 90 "...there were three of us ..." http://, op.cit..

p. 91 "...playing Ping-Pong with me ..." *Newsweek*, March 11, 1996, p.26.

p. 92 "I've been in a privileged position ..." *A Tribute to Princess Diana*, op.cit., p.71

p. 92 "They kept saying I was manipulative ..." *The New Yorker*, Sept. 15, 1997, p.58.

p. 92 "But William—I think he ..." Ibid.

p. 93 "We would have been the best ..." *The New Yorker*, op. cit., p.59.

CHAPTER EIGHT

p. 94 "She was the people's princess." *Time*, Sept. 8. 1997, p.37.

p. 95 "...any sane person would ..." *Newsweek*, Sept. 8, 1997, p.35.

p. 96 "She was the people's princess." *Time*, Sept. 8, 1997, p.37.

p. 97 "...every editor of every publication..." *Newsweek*, Sept. 8, 1997, p.34.

p. 97 "...and not one tear has been shed ..." Buskin, op.cit., p.220.

p. 97 "...the Royal Family have been hurt ..." *Newsweek*, Sept. 15, 1997, p.36.

p. 98 "I want to pay tribute ..." *Newsweek*, Sept. 15,1997, p.21.

p. 99 "Above all, we give thanks ..." op.cit., p.29.

p. 99 "Diana profoundly influenced ...": op.cit., p.30.

p. 99 "Your footsteps will always fall ..." op.cit., p.33.

Index